CAMPAIGN 378

LEYTE GULF 1944 (2)

Surigao Strait and Cape Engaño

MARK STILLE

ILLUSTRATED BY JIM LAURIER
Series editor Nikolai Bogdanovic

OSPREY PUBLISHING
Bloomsbury Publishing Plc
PO Box 883, Oxford, OX1 9PL, UK
29 Earlsfort Terrace, Dublin 2, Ireland
1385 Broadway, 5th Floor, New York, NY 10018, USA
E-mail: info@ospreypublishing.com
www.ospreypublishing.com

OSPREY is a trademark of Osprey Publishing Ltd

First published in Great Britain in 2022

A catalog record for this book is available from the British Library.

ISBN: PB 9781472842855; eBook 9781472842862; ePDF 9781472842831; XML 9781472842848

22 23 24 25 26   10 9 8 7 6 5 4 3 2 1

Maps by www.bounford.com
3D BEVs by Paul Kime
Index by Alison Worthington
Typeset by PDQ Digital Media Solutions, Bungay, UK
Printed and bound in India by Replika Press Private Ltd.

Artist's note

Readers can find out more about the work of illustrator Jim Laurier via the following website:
www.jimlaurier.com

Osprey Publishing supports the Woodland Trust, the UK's leading woodland conservation charity.

To find out more about our authors and books visit **www.ospreypublishing.com**. Here you will find extracts, author interviews, details of forthcoming events and the option to sign up for our newsletter.

Photographs

All the photographs that appear in this work are US Public Domain.

Japanese names

In this work, Japanese names are presented with the forename first, followed by the family name.

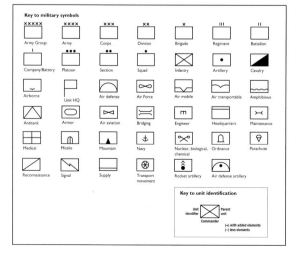

Front cover illustration: The Japanese fleet carrier *Zuikaku* under air attack on October 25, 1944. (Jim Laurier)

Title page photo: Heavy cruiser *Nachi* (Admiral Shima's flagship) under attack from aircraft from TG 38.3 in Manila Bay on November 5, 1944.

CONTENTS

The Philippines and locations of principal USN and IJN forces

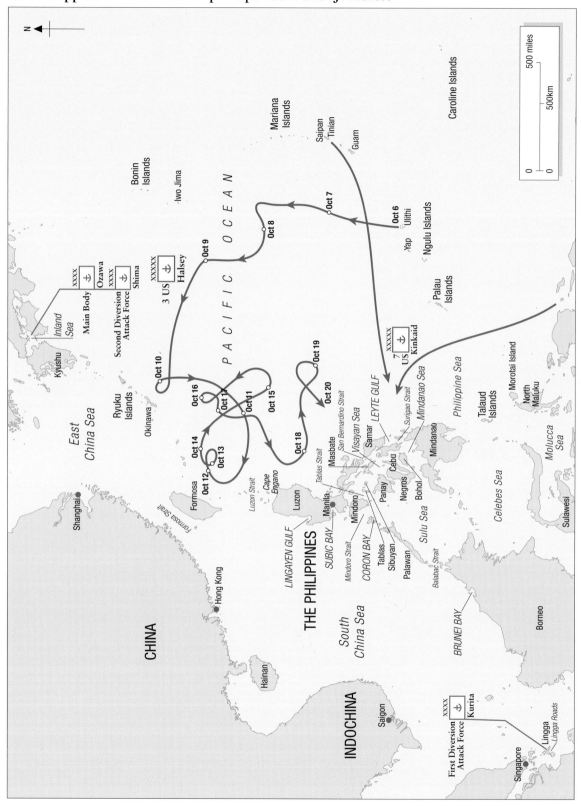

INTRODUCTION

The Battle of Leyte Gulf was the largest naval clash in history. It was actually four major actions conducted over the course of two days with several other smaller associated actions. The size and complexity of the battle is unmatched. The United States Navy (USN) employed two fleets, the Third and the Seventh, with a total of over 220 principal combatants (destroyer size and larger). Among these were 34 aircraft carriers of all types, 12 battleships, and an array of cruisers and destroyers. This imposing collection of warships was sent to Leyte to escort an invasion force of 420 amphibious ships carrying 132,400 men.

Facing the might of the USN was a much-reduced Imperial Japanese Navy (IJN). Because the Japanese judged that the fall of the Philippines would fatally compromise their ability to continue the war, since American control would cut off Japanese sea lines of communications (SLOC) with the resource areas of Southeast Asia, the IJN planned to make a supreme effort to defeat the invasion of Leyte. This effort was given the designation *Sho-Go*, or *Victory Operation*. However, even with its determination to throw everything it had into the fight, the IJN was severely outnumbered and was fatally weak in airpower. A combined force of 69 combatants was mustered for the operation, broken down into four main forces. Unlike in previous major battles when the IJN's main strength was its carrier force, *Sho-Go* was built around a scheme to get the bulk of the IJN's remaining battleships and heavy cruisers to attack the American beachhead on Leyte. To give the heavy ships this opportunity, the IJN's remaining carriers were slated to be used as a diversion to draw the USN's powerful Third Fleet away from Leyte. Though clever, *Sho-Go* had no chance of success, even if it would have unfolded as intended.

The unparalleled size of the forces committed and the complexity of the battles they fought, combined with the alluring but totally false notion that the IJN still had a chance to wrest victory from the jaws of defeat as late as October 1944, generate endless fascination with the Battle of Leyte Gulf. This is the second of two Osprey Campaigns covering the battle. The first book focused on the operations of the IJN's First Diversion Attack Force as it steamed toward Leyte Gulf to attack the invasion force. Along the way it fought two major battles—the Battle of the Sibuyan Sea on October 24 when the Japanese were subjected to heavy air attack from the Third Fleet, and the Battle off Samar on October 25 when the still-powerful First Diversion Attack Force headed south toward Leyte Gulf and encountered a group of USN escort carriers. Following the action off Samar, the Japanese

The dominant force during the Battle of Leyte Gulf was TF 38. This is TG 38.2 maneuvering on October 25, 1944 when it launched a series of attacks on Ozawa's Main Body. Visible are fleet carriers *Intrepid* and *Bunker Hill* and light carriers *Cabot* and *Independence*.

commander decided not to attack into Leyte Gulf but to retreat. This ended any prospect of even a Pyrrhic IJN victory.

This book focuses on the IJN forces supporting the main thrust of the First Diversion Attack Force. The most important of these was the Main Body, the IJN's punchless carrier force, with the mission of luring the Third Fleet to the north. At the Battle off Cape Engaño, the Main Body succeeded in its mission but at a tremendous cost. The decision of the commander of the Third Fleet, the aggressive Admiral William F. Halsey, was clearly the most controversial and consequential of the battle and deserves careful examination. Also assisting the First Diversion Attack Force was a small detachment of seven ships built around two old battleships that were ordered to attack into Leyte Gulf through Surigao Strait in the south while the First Diversion Attack Force entered the gulf from the north. The resulting Battle of Surigao Strait on October 25 featured the last battleship duel in history.

ORIGINS OF THE CAMPAIGN

In June 1944, the Americans attacked the Mariana Islands. To repel this advance into their inner defensive zone, the Japanese fought what they hoped would be a decisive battle. In fact, the battle was decisive but not in the way the Japanese had envisioned. The IJN's carefully rebuilt carrier force was defeated, losing virtually all its trained aviators and three carriers. The Americans then proceeded to capture Saipan, Tinian, and Guam. Loss of the Marianas meant that the Japanese Home Islands were within range of American B-29 bombers.

Having secured the Marianas, the Americans planned their next operation with the objective of cutting Japan off from critical resources in Southeast Asia. Two main choices emerged for the next target. General Douglas MacArthur, Supreme Commander Southwest Pacific Area, wanted to hit the Philippines. Admiral Chester Nimitz and his boss, Admiral Ernest King, preferred to bypass the Philippines and invade Formosa and the Chinese coast. A late July conference at Pearl Harbor, overseen by President Franklin Roosevelt, between Nimitz and MacArthur did not resolve the issue.

The actual decision was rendered by the Joint Chiefs of Staff, which came up with a compromise plan. It called for an initial lodgment in the Philippines to establish air bases. This would be accomplished by invading Mindanao in November. From there, Leyte would be next with a planned invasion date of December 20, 1944. Subsequent operations were left open—it was undetermined if the main Philippine island of Luzon would be invaded or bypassed. MacArthur was smart enough to realize that once the Central Philippines were liberated the momentum to clear Luzon would be unstoppable.

This compromise plan was thrown into confusion by real-world events. As the Third Fleet ravaged Japanese defenses in the Philippines preparing for the invasion of Mindanao, Halsey assessed that the weak state of Japanese resistance brought an opportunity to move up the operational schedule and thereby shorten the war. His proposal on September 13 was bold: with the Third Fleet providing air cover, the invasion of Mindanao could be skipped, and Leyte targeted in October. This had the support of MacArthur and with the prospect of speeding up the tempo of operations, it was quickly approved by the Joint Chiefs. The resulting directive set the landing date on Leyte as October 20.

The Japanese position had become increasingly desperate after the Battle of the Philippine Sea in June 1944 and the fall of Saipan. Not only had their inner defensive line been penetrated, but also the IJN was decisively

Nimitz and MacArthur had competing visions of the best path for the American advance in the Pacific during 1944. Here they discuss strategy at MacArthur's headquarters in Brisbane, Australia on March 27, 1944. The landing on Leyte in October reflected MacArthur's vision.

defeated. This defeat was so comprehensive that it compromised any ability to successfully defend Japan's final defensive line. The Battle of the Philippine Sea marked the effective end of the IJN's carrier force. There was no hope that it could be rebuilt before the following American offensive. This meant that the next battle would be fought primarily by surface ships with whatever help land-based air forces could render.

As the Americans decided on the location and timing of their next advance, the Japanese correctly deduced that the target would be Leyte. They remained unclear as to the timing of any American assault, but finally settled on the last ten days of October. The *Sho-1* variant of *Sho-Go* planned for this contingency.

Even before the first American troops splashed ashore on Leyte on October 20, the first phase of the Battle of Leyte Gulf had already concluded. In response to a series of pre-invasion strikes by the Third Fleet, including strikes on Formosa beginning on October 12, the IJN activated the land-based air forces for *Sho-1* and *Sho-2* (defense of Formosa). The commander of the Combined Fleet, Admiral Soemu Toyoda, assessed that this was a favorable opportunity to inflict severe damage on the Third Fleet. He committed all available air forces, including the nearly trained air groups of the IJN's carriers, to fly from land bases.

In one of the largest air battles of the war, Halsey's carriers struck targets on Formosa with over 2,500 sorties from October 12 to 14. The Japanese responded by massing some 1,400 aircraft to attack the Third Fleet. However, only 761 offensive sorties were directed at the American carriers, beginning on the evening of October 12. Against the radar-directed fighters of the Third Fleet, the poorly coordinated Japanese attacks stood little chance of success. The Japanese admitted to losing 321 aircraft, but this did not stop Japanese aviators from claiming 11 carriers sunk; in fact, not a single USN carrier was even damaged. Toyoda was hopeful the battle had at least delayed the American attack. In fact, the battle had reduced the IJN's land-based air forces to ineffectiveness on the eve of the American invasion.

CHRONOLOGY

1944

October 17	Japanese spot USN forces on eastern approaches to Leyte Gulf and place *Sho-1* forces on alert.
October 18	Japanese give the execute order for *Sho-1*.
October 20	US forces land on Leyte.
	Main Body departs Japan.
October 22	Nishimura's force departs Brunei Bay.
October 24	0918hrs: TG 38.4 attacks Nishimura's force; *Fuso* is hit by a bomb, but damage is light.
	1115hrs: Main Body detects TG 38.3 and launches an air strike.
	1635hrs: Main Body is spotted by Task Force (TF) 38 aircraft.
	1950hrs: Halsey orders TF 38 north to attack Main Body.
	2236hrs: *PT-131* gains first contact on Nishimura's force approaching Surigao Strait.
October 25	0213hrs: last PT boat attack on Nishimura's force; no Japanese ships are hit.
	0240hrs: first radar contact on Nishimura's force by USN destroyers.
	0300hrs: USN destroyers launch first torpedo attack.
	0308hrs: two torpedoes hit *Fuso*.
	0310hrs: second torpedo attack launched.
	0319hrs: three IJN destroyers are hit by torpedoes; one sinks immediately, one within minutes, one survives but falls out of formation. *Yamashiro* is also hit.
	0323hrs: third torpedo attack launched with no success.
	0325hrs: *Abukuma* hit by PT torpedo.
	0329–0336hrs: fourth torpedo attack launched.
	0331hrs: *Yamashiro* is hit by a torpedo.
	0345hrs: *Fuso* sinks.
	0351hrs: USN cruisers open fire on *Yamashiro*.
	0353hrs: USN battleships open fire on *Yamashiro*.

0407–0411hrs: three torpedoes from fifth USN destroyer attack hit *Yamashiro*.

0409hrs: Oldendorf orders ceasefire.

0411hrs: *Yamshiro* capsizes.

0422hrs: Shima's two heavy cruisers each fire eight torpedoes.

0425hrs: Shima orders his force to withdraw.

0710hrs: Main Body is spotted by TF 38 aircraft.

0830hrs: first air attack on Main Body damages *Zuikaku* and *Zuiho* and cripples *Chitose*.

0847hrs: Kinkaid orders Oldendorf north to assist escort carriers.

0937hrs: *Chitose* sinks.

0945hrs: second air strike on Main Body cripples *Chiyoda*.

1115hrs: TF 34 and TG 38.2 head south to assist escort carriers.

1242hrs: *Abukuma* sinks after B-24 attack.

1307hrs: *Mogami* sinks.

1310–1400hrs: third air strike hits Main Body.

1414hrs: *Zuikaku* sinks.

1445hrs: fourth air strike hits Main Body focusing on *Ise* and *Hyuga*.

1526hrs: *Zuiho* sinks.

1655hrs: *Chiyoda* sunk by cruiser gunfire.

1710–1740hrs: fifth air strike hits Main Body; *Ise* and *Hyuga* are lightly damaged.

1810hrs: sixth air strike inflicts no damage on Main Body.

2004hrs: submarine *Jallao* sinks *Tama*.

2059hrs: destroyer *Hatsuzuki* sunk by USN cruiser and destroyer gunfire.

2130hrs: USN breaks off pursuit of Main Body.

October 26   0100hrs: TG 34.5 arrives off San Bernardino Strait.

0132hrs: destroyer *Nowaki* sunk by USN gunfire south of San Bernardino Strait.

OPPOSING COMMANDERS

UNITED STATES NAVY

General Douglas MacArthur, in his capacity as Supreme Commander Southwest Pacific Area, commanded the ground forces, most supporting air forces, and the Seventh Fleet. Reflecting command friction between the Army and the Navy, MacArthur ordered that all communications between the Seventh Fleet and the Third Fleet go through his headquarters instead of directly to each other.

Overall direction of USN strategy and worldwide resource allocation was under the direction of **Admiral Ernest J. King** in his capacities as Commander in Chief, US Fleet and Chief of Naval Operations. **Admiral Chester W. Nimitz**, Commander in Chief Pacific Fleet and Pacific Ocean Areas, retained strategic control of the Third Fleet.

Admiral William F. Halsey was the single-most important command figure in the battle, since the powerful Third Fleet was under his direct authority. Halsey was a 1904 graduate of the Naval Academy and a destroyer sailor early in his career. The Chief of the Bureau of Aeronautics, Ernest King, offered him command of carrier *Saratoga* in 1934. Since carrier commanders had to be qualified naval aviators, Halsey attended a 12-week aviation course set up for senior commanders and earned his aviator's wings in May 1935 at the age of 52. This made him the USN's most senior carrier division commander at the start of World War II. Early in the war, Halsey made his mark as an extremely aggressive commander by conducting a series of carrier raids on Japanese bases. The final raid was against Tokyo in April 1942. As a carrier commander, he longed to get a crack at the Japanese carrier force, but this never happened until October 1944 at Leyte Gulf. He missed

Admiral William Halsey and members of his staff in conference aboard *New Jersey*, December 1944. Halsey's staff did not serve him well on a number of occasions, one example being on October 24/25 when Halsey had to decide what to do against several approaching Japanese naval forces.

Vice Admiral Marc Mitscher, commander of TF 38 and the premier practitioner of carrier warfare in the world in October 1944, was sidelined by Halsey for most of the battle. Halsey would have been better served by seeking Mitscher's guidance and then seriously considering it on October 24/25.

the carrier battle at Coral Sea because of the Tokyo Raid and then missed Midway because of a skin disease. After his recovery, he assumed command of Allied forces at Guadalcanal. He succeeded in turning Allied fortunes around using the aggressiveness for which he was famous. Following victory at Guadalcanal, Halsey directed operations in the Central and Northern Solomons. In May 1944, Halsey was given command of the Third Fleet. Though not present at the Battle of the Philippine Sea, he thought that the USN victory was incomplete, since the bulk of the IJN's carrier force had escaped destruction. He was determined not to make the same mistake at Leyte Gulf when the Japanese carrier force again showed itself.

Vice Admiral Marc Mitscher was the commander of TF 38, the Third Fleet's Fast Carrier Force. Mitscher was the most experienced practitioner of large-scale carrier operations in the world by October 1944. He and Halsey had a fractious relationship. Halsey and his staff often took it upon themselves to act as a task force, rather than as fleet commanders. This tendency to micromanage undermined Mitscher's responsibilities and reduced his initiative. TF 38 was comprised of four subordinate task groups. Each was commanded by experienced and capable officers. Task Group (TG) 38.1 was under **Vice Admiral John S. McCain**; TG 38.2 was led by **Rear Admiral Gerald F. Bogan**; TG 38.3 by **Rear Admiral Frederick C. Sherman**; and TG 38.4 was commanded by **Rear Admiral Ralph E. Davison**. If a fleet engagement with the IJN was a possibility, a separate task group built around TF 38's battleships was formed into a separate battle line. Designated TF 34, it was commanded by **Vice Admiral Willis A. Lee**, who was considered the USN's leading gunnery expert.

Commander of the Seventh Fleet was **Vice Admiral Thomas C. Kinkaid**. His career began in 1908 after graduating from Annapolis. In 1937, he

Commander of the Seventh Fleet, Vice Admiral Thomas Kinkaid, watches landing operations in Lingayen Gulf from the bridge of his flagship, January 1945. At Leyte Gulf, Kinkaid's performance was uneven, which was a contributing factor to exposing some of his forces to heavy attack.

gained command of heavy cruiser *Indianapolis*. This led to command of a cruiser division immediately after the Pacific War began. Present at both Coral Sea and Midway, he commanded a carrier task force at the start of the Guadalcanal campaign. His record as a carrier task force commander was poor, and as a non-aviator, Kinkaid did not receive another carrier command after the Battle of Santa Cruz in October 1942. In January 1943 he was sent to a back-water command in the North Pacific and was ordered to improve relations with US Army commands in the area. Kinkaid's ability to work with the Army resurrected his career. This set him up for the much more important billet as Commander, Allied Naval Forces Southwest Pacific Area and Commander of the Seventh Fleet. The Seventh Fleet became known as "MacArthur's Navy" because of its string of successful amphibious operations in the New Guinea area. Kinkaid had a mixed record at Leyte Gulf. He oversaw preparations for the Battle of Surigao Strait, but also allowed his escort carriers to be surprised by Japanese surface forces. Halsey is usually given full blame for this, but Kinkaid shared some of the responsibility.

Direct air cover for the Seventh Fleet was provided by TG 77.4 under command of **Rear Admiral Thomas L. Sprague**, who was also in direct command of one group of escort carriers commonly known as "Taffy 1." "Taffy 2" was under the command of **Rear Admiral Felix B. Stump**. "Taffy 3" was led by **Rear Admiral Clifton A.F. Sprague**, who took the brunt of the Japanese attack during the Battle off Samar and performed brilliantly under extreme duress.

The Northern and Southern Attack Forces were each responsible for delivering one of MacArthur's corps to the invasion beaches on Leyte. Supporting the landings was the Bombardment and Fire Support Group

ABOVE LEFT
Vice Admiral Willis Lee yearned to get the battleships of TF 34 within range of the Japanese fleet. His best chance to pull this off was at Leyte Gulf, but developments denied him the opportunity to see his battleships in action against the Japanese.

ABOVE RIGHT
Jessie Oldendorf as a vice admiral aboard battleship *Tennessee* off Okinawa, August 1945. Oldendorf had the distinction of commanding the largest force of USN battleships ever to engage in a surface action. He fought a solid, though not flawless, battle at Surigao Strait.

under **Rear Admiral Jessie B. Oldendorf**. He was a 1909 Annapolis graduate. Early in the war he was given assignments in the Atlantic theater, but in January 1944 he was placed in command of Cruiser Division 4 and saw action in a number of Pacific invasions throughout the year. As the most senior of Kinkaid's admirals, he was assigned responsibility for planning the American side of the Battle of Surigao Strait. Oldendorf's principal subordinates were **Rear Admiral G.L. Weyler** and **Rear Admiral R.S. Berkey**.

IMPERIAL JAPANESE NAVY

The IJN's principal force was the Combined Fleet, which since May 1944 was under the command of **Admiral Soemu Toyoda**. He was viewed as an experienced and intelligent officer by his subordinates, but this reputation did him no good in 1944 as he planned the decisive battles at Philippine Sea and then at Leyte Gulf. Toyoda approved the sound plan that he inherited for the Philippine Sea battle and then formulated his own plan at Leyte Gulf. This plan was deeply flawed, as will be detailed below.

The Combined Fleet's principal command was the Mobile Force under the command of **Vice Admiral Jisaburo Ozawa**. At Leyte Gulf he was in direct command of the Main Body that was composed of the IJN's remaining carriers. Ozawa was one of the IJN's most capable officers and performed well during the war. He was an airpower advocate who had held the job of Combined Fleet chief of staff before the war. Ozawa was

entrusted with the task of overseeing the naval forces that were ordered to seize the southern resource areas at the start of the war. In November 1942, he assumed command of the IJN's carrier force, and held this job up until Leyte Gulf. At Philippine Sea, he wielded his carriers as well as anybody could have done, but he was outclassed by USN technical and numerical superiority. His performance at Leyte Gulf was professional, though he expected to lose his entire force in the course of acting as a decoy.

The most important IJN command figure at Leyte Gulf was **Vice Admiral Takeo Kurita**, commander of the First Diversion Attack Force. This force was part of Mobile Force and thus under Ozawa's command, but was separated geographically and thus proceeded independently. Kurita faced long odds to accomplish his mission, but he made them longer with a weak performance in the Battle off Samar. When deciding whether to press on into Leyte Gulf, which would have almost certainly resulted in the total destruction of his force, Kurita made the courageous decision to retreat instead of executing Toyoda's hopeless plan to the very end.

Vice Admiral Takeo Kurita led the principal IJN force during the battle. It is all but certain he never believed in the plan he was ordered to execute, and when given the opportunity, he declined to lead his command to utter destruction.

Vice Admiral Shoji Nishimura commanded the detached portion of the First Diversion Attack Force ordered to attack into Leyte Gulf through Surigao Strait. Born in 1889, he graduated from Etajima in 1911. Originally a navigation expert, he switched to torpedoes as his area of expertise. Nishimura spent the vast majority of his career at sea and detested time ashore. He attended the Naval Staff College from 1936 to 1938; to be eligible for flag officer, he was allowed to take the Naval Staff College exams without completing all the classes. Even after his Naval Staff College experience, or perhaps because of it, Nishimura was disdainful of the "armchair strategists" and was more comfortable at sea.

Being the "sea dog" that he was, Nishimura had extensive, but uneven, combat experience. He began the war in command of Destroyer Squadron 4. He carried out his duties aggressively but with mixed results. At the Battle of Balikpapan in February 1942, the invasion force he was escorting was attacked by USN destroyers that sank several transports before getting away unscathed. In July 1942 Nishimura was in command of a squadron of heavy cruisers that conducted an ineffectual bombardment of Henderson Field on Guadalcanal on the night of November 14. In spite of his checkered combat record, he was promoted to vice admiral. After a brief period ashore, Nishimura was assigned to take over Battleship Division 2 in September 1944. This unit was comprised of the IJN's two most outdated battleships.

Nishimura exhibited a determined, if fatalistic, attitude at Leyte Gulf. His two battleships were seen as expendable and were detached from Kurita's main body as a decoy. Nishimura knew his small command would probably be annihilated, but he was determined to carry out his diversion mission if it contributed to Kurita's success. His actions have been criticized as rash, but they must be seen through the lens of this objective.

Vice Admiral Shoji Nishimura was also charged with assisting the main attack by Kurita's First Diversion Attack Force. To do this, he adhered to the original plan and schedule for his small force, which led to its near-total destruction at Surigao Strait.

Instead of being seen as foolish, by all accounts from both subordinates and superiors, he was a serious and studious man who considered all options during planning.

Japanese naval forces in the Philippines were under the command of the Southwest Area Fleet led by **Vice Admiral Guinichi Mikawa**. He was an experienced commander who began the war as a commander of battleships in the IJN's carrier force and then assumed command of the Eighth Fleet in Rabaul and played a central role during the Guadalcanal campaign. His victory at Savo Island in August 1942 handed the USN one of its worst defeats of the war. **Vice Admiral Kiyohide Shima** led the Second Diversion Attack Force that was under Mikawa's command, even though it was operating in the same area and had the same objective as Nishimura's force. Shima graduated in 1911 from Etajima as a classmate of Nishimura, but by October 1944 he was senior to Nishimura. His career specialty was in communications. Unlike Nishimura, he was not a sea dog, as most of his career had been spent on staff assignments. During the war, he commanded two cruiser divisions before being promoted to vice admiral in May 1943. In February 1944, he was given command of the Fifth Fleet, which was responsible for defending the northern approaches to Japan. His contemporaries saw him in several ways. One stated, clearly after the fact, that he was a gentle man well suited to staff work, but as a fleet commander he was found wanting, especially in chaotic night battles. Another indicated that he possessed a forceful character. Both sides were in evidence in October 1944. He fought hard to have his small force included in the attack into Leyte Gulf that more than likely would become a one-way operation. When given the opportunity, he did little with it.

OPPOSING FLEETS

The tide of war had firmly turned against Japan by October 1944. In almost three years of war, the IJN had taken heavy losses. Wedded to the notion that decisive battles decided wars, the IJN had retained the bulk of its pre-war battleships and heavy cruiser fleets. Even by this late stage of the war, 9 of 12 battleships and 14 of 18 heavy cruisers remained. Missing was the bulk of the carrier force which had fought hard in the war's five carrier battles. Toyoda decided to throw virtually every ship in the Combined Fleet into *Sho-1*, but Table 1 shows the naval balance was still dramatically against the Japanese.

Table 1: Total naval forces employed at Leyte Gulf

	IJN	USN
Airpower		
Fleet carriers	1	8
Light carriers	3	8
Escort carriers	0	18
Total carrier aircraft	116	1,500
Land-based aircraft	approx. 350 operational on October 24	0
Surface combatants		
Battleships	9	12
Heavy cruisers	14	13
Light cruisers	7	15
Destroyers	35	147
Destroyer escorts	0	14
Total combatants	69	235

As the IJN grew weaker, the USN grew stronger. Table 1 shows the impact of American wartime production, but it fails to impart the qualitative edge possessed by the USN in almost all aspects of naval warfare.

Since this volume focuses on the Battle of Surigao Strait and the Battle off Cape Engaño, only those forces engaged in those actions will be examined.

UNITED STATES NAVY

THIRD FLEET

The principal USN striking force in the Pacific was Halsey's Third Fleet. It contained all the USN's fast carriers and most modern battleships. The carrier

portion of the fleet was designated TF 38 and in accordance with well-tested doctrine, TF 38 was broken down into four task groups. Each task group was assigned one, two, or three fleet carriers and two light carriers. Each possessed a strong escort of up to two battleships, two to four cruisers, and a variable number of destroyers. Though carrier aircraft were TF 38's main weapon, American admirals still saw an important role for the fleet's battleships. If a fleet action seemed imminent, the battleships were pulled from the various task forces and formed into a separate battle line with a cruiser and destroyer escort. Formation of TF 34, as the battleships were designated, was done to finish off any Japanese ships crippled by carrier strikes, but ideally to catch and engage the IJN's battle line.

Essex-class carrier *Franklin* pictured shortly after being completed in February 1944. Assigned to TG 38.4, she launched strikes against Nishimura's force on October 24 and against Ozawa's force the next day.

Fleet and light carriers

Eight USN fleet carriers participated in the battle. Seven of these were new Essex-class ships, which had begun to arrive in the Pacific in August 1943. These were the most powerful ships of the war with a fine blend of striking power, speed, endurance, and defensive capabilities. They possessed unmatched offensive capabilities in the form of an air group of up to 100 aircraft. The veteran *Enterprise* was slightly smaller, but it still carried an air group of some 90 aircraft. Supporting the fleet carriers were eight Independence-class light carriers. Each embarked an air group of 34 aircraft.

Light carrier *Langley* anchored in Ulithi harbor in the Caroline Islands on October 31, 1944, following the Battle of Leyte Gulf. Essex-class carrier *Hornet* is among the many ships in the background. The light carrier air groups were comprised mostly of fighters; their main mission was usually fleet air defense to allow the Essex-class air groups to focus on offensive operations.

Flight deck crews remove a wounded pilot from his F6F Hellcat after one of the strikes against Ozawa's force on October 25, 1944. The scene took place on *Lexington*.

Carrier air groups and aircraft

At Leyte Gulf, an Essex-class carrier air group was comprised of a 36-aircraft fighter squadron, a 36-aircraft dive-bomber squadron, and a torpedo squadron with 18 aircraft. Each light carrier embarked an air group of 25 fighters and 9 torpedo planes.

USN fleet and light carriers operated three types of aircraft. The standard carrier fighter was the Grumman F6F-3 Hellcat. It was far superior to its Japanese counterpart the Mitsubishi A6M "Zero" by virtue of advantages in protection, speed, and firepower. In addition to flying superior airplanes, USN fighter pilots were much better trained and more experienced than all but a few of their Japanese adversaries.

The standard dive-bomber was the Curtiss SB2C Helldiver, which had finally replaced the well-loved Douglas SBD Dauntless after a prolonged and painful gestation period. The SB2C-3 version was fast (with a top speed of almost 300mph), rugged, and could carry a bomb load of 1,000lb.

A division of SB2C Helldivers in formation. By October 1944, the Helldiver was the only dive-bomber flying from USN carriers. Following a long gestation period, the Helldiver proved itself to be a very capable dive-bomber that eventually accounted for more Japanese ships than any other type of Allied aircraft. However, it lacked the killing power to sink large Japanese warships, but it was deadly against smaller and unarmored ships.

The best torpedo bomber of the war was the Grumman TBF/TBM Avenger. Reliable in service, and able to withstand battle damage, the Avenger could operate as a torpedo plane or a conventional bomber. The standard USN air-launched torpedo was the Mark 13, which had proven chronically unreliable during the first two years of the war. By 1944 these issues had finally been rectified so that the Avenger could conduct a more survivable attack profile at up to 270mph at an altitude of up to 800ft. A functioning torpedo greatly enhanced the ship-killing capabilities of American carrier air groups and was essential if carriers hoped to sink heavily armored IJN ships.

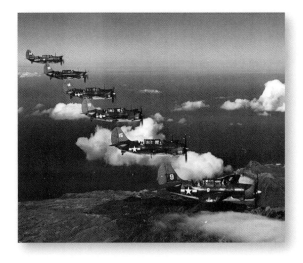

Carrier air group tactics

Each USN carrier air group conducted morning and afternoon searches in accordance with the task group's overall reconnaissance plan. Under normal operational conditions, the search range of USN carrier aircraft was about 325NM. The typical strike range of a carrier air group was much less, usually about 200NM based on a range of tactical conditions. USN carrier air groups trained intensively to conduct attacks on ships, but TF 38's operations over the months before the battle were primarily against land targets. This meant that the skills required to attack maritime targets had atrophied. A much more serious problem was aircrew fatigue. The pace of operations leading to the Leyte invasion was relentless, and once the IJN made an appearance, aircrews were ordered to fly two or three missions for several consecutive days, which made fatigue a real issue.

Earlier in the war, USN carrier air groups experienced significant issues with fragmented strikes and the lack of a functioning torpedo. By 1944, these problems had been overcome and USN carrier air groups possessed a proven doctrine for attacking Japanese naval targets. Each carrier's air group conducted its attack separately under the direction of an overall strike coordinator, whose job it was to allocate targets to each air group, thus hopefully eliminating overconcentration on a single target or a situation where a key target was left untouched.

When an air group conducted its attack, the goal was to coordinate the actions of the fighters, dive-bombers, and torpedo planes to overwhelm the target's defenses. As per doctrine, the Helldivers attacked first using a standard dive-bombing profile consisting of a shallow approach from 20,000ft followed by a steep 65–70° dive from between 15,000 and 12,000ft. The 1,000lb bomb carried aboard the Helldivers was typically released at 1,500–2,000ft above the target. Usually, the Helldiver squadron was divided into divisions of six aircraft to enable attacks on different targets or to overwhelm one target from several different directions. The target ship was attacked along its longitudinal axis to present the largest target possible. The Japanese tried to counter this with an evasion tactic of steering a complete circle to present the dive-bomber pilots with a constantly changing target axis. The main purpose of dive-bomber attacks on large warships was to reduce their defenses for follow-up torpedo attacks. Supporting the Helldivers, Hellcat fighters conducted low-level strafing attacks on target ships to kill antiaircraft gun crews. Once the target's defenses had been reduced, Avengers commenced their torpedo runs. Attacking torpedo bombers were broken into two sections to conduct an "anvil" attack, with Avengers approaching the target simultaneously from both bows, making it difficult for the target to maneuver without exposing itself to attack from at least one of the sections.

Surface combatants

Often overlooked because it seldom got the opportunity to engage Japanese ships, is TF 38's powerful force of surface combatants. These ships provided effective antiaircraft support to the carriers, but it also possessed significant capabilities against surface ships. In October 1944, TF 38's battle line consisted of six battleships, all commissioned after 1941. All carried 16in. guns and the best fire-control systems afloat. Protection against air and surface attack was of the highest order. *Washington* was a North Carolina-class ship mounting nine 16in./45 guns and 20 5in./38 dual-purpose guns with a top speed of 28 knots. *Alabama*, *Massachusetts*, and *South Dakota* were three of the four ships of the South Dakota class. They also carried a main battery of nine 16in./45 guns and were better protected than the preceding North Carolina class, but they were slightly slower. *Iowa* and *New Jersey* were the first two ships of the Iowa class, which was the only USN battleship class built without restrictions imposed by pre-war naval treaties. The Iowa class emphasized speed (top speed 33 knots), but at over 57,000 tons full load displacement it was big enough to carry heavy protection and a main battery of nine 16in./50 guns. It should be emphasized that all modern USN battleships were better protected and better armed than any Japanese battleship, except for the two Yamato-class ships.

The battleship *New Jersey*, in 1944. She and sistership *Iowa* were assigned to TF 38 during the Battle of Leyte Gulf, but they never had an opportunity to engage a Japanese ship. *New Jersey* served as Halsey's flagship during the battle.

TF 38 also possessed two types of heavy cruisers, all armed with 8in. guns. The pre-war "Treaty" cruisers made significant compromises in protection, but the Baltimore class, completed during the war, was a balanced design and was the best heavy cruiser afloat. Light cruisers assigned to TF 38 included Atlanta-class ships best suited for antiaircraft duties and the 10,000-ton Cleveland class that carried a formidable main battery of 12 6in. guns with a high rate of fire. The Cleveland class was the best light cruiser of the war. By October 1944, the standard USN fleet destroyer was the Fletcher class. These balanced ships possessed high speed and a main battery of five 5in./38 guns and ten torpedo tubes.

SEVENTH FLEET

Kinkaid's Seventh Fleet was responsible for the immediate protection of the invasion force from air, surface, and submarine attack. To accomplish this, some 130 principal combatants were assigned to the Seventh Fleet. The most powerful were allocated to Oldendorf and fought at the Battle of Surigao Strait. Their primary characteristics are outlined in Table 2.

Battleships

Of the six old USN battleships present at Surigao Strait, five had been at Pearl Harbor on December 7, 1941. All six had been modernized since the beginning of the war, and three had been extensively rebuilt after being damaged at Pearl Harbor and possessed firepower capabilities equal to the modern battleships assigned to TF 38. However, all old USN battleships were much slower than their Japanese counterparts, and most had severe deficiencies with underwater protection.

Table 2: Characteristics of Seventh Fleet warships at the Battle of Surigao Strait

Ship	Tonnage (full load)	Principal weapons	Main armor	Top speed
Battleships				
Maryland, West Virginia	33,590	8 16in. guns, 16 5in./38 dual-purpose (DP) guns (Maryland 6 5in./25 DP, 10 5in./51)	main belt 16in., horizontal 7.9–9.1 in.	21 knots
California, Tennessee	40,345	12 14in./50, 16 5in./38 dual-purpose guns	main belt 13.5in., horizontal 7–8in.	20.5 knots
Mississippi	33,000	12 14in./50, 8 5in./25 DP, 6 5in./51	main belt 13.5in., horizontal 6.75in.	21 knots
Pennsylvania	32,567	12 14in./45, 16 5in./38 DP	main belt 13.5in.; horizontal 6.25in.	21 knots
Heavy cruisers				
Louisville, Portland, Minneapolis	11,420–12,493	9 8in./55, eight 5in./25 DP	main belt between 3 and 5.75in.; horizontal between 1 and 2.5in.	32.5 knots
Shropshire (Royal Australian Navy (RAN))	13,315	8 8in., 4 4in.	main belt 4.5in., horizontal 1.375in.	32 knots
Light cruisers				
Boise, Phoenix	12,207	15 6in./47, 8 5in./25 DP	main belt 5.37in., horizontal 2in.	32.5 knots
Columbia, Denver	14,131	12 6in./47, 12 5in./38 DP	main belt 5in., horizontal 2in.	32.5 knots
Destroyers				
Fletcher class (28)	2,500	5 5in./38, 10 21in. torpedo tubes	none	36.5 knots
Tribal class (RAN) (1)	2,122	6 4.7in., 4 21in. torpedo tubes	none	36.5 knots

West Virginia suffered severe damage at Pearl Harbor and was rebuilt. This view is from July 1944 after her reconstruction. Note the new 5in./38 mounts on the beam. The large radar on the top of the forward superstructure is an SK air search radar. Below it is the cylindrical Mk 8 radar on top of the main battery fire control director. A second Mark 34 main battery director is visible abaft the mainmast.

Maryland and *West Virginia* were two of the USN's three pre-war battleships equipped with 16in. guns. *Maryland* was only lightly modernized before October 1944, but *West Virginia* had been rebuilt. *Tennessee* and *California* were also damaged at Pearl Harbor, and both were also rebuilt. The original main battery of 12 14in. guns was retained, but fire control capabilities were dramatically upgraded with the addition of two Mark 34 main battery directors each with the Mark 8 fire control radar. The old casemate-mounted secondary battery was removed and replaced with a battery of 16 dual-purpose 5in./38 guns in eight twin mounts. Torpedo protection was enhanced with the addition of a torpedo blister and more internal longitudinal bulkheads. Horizontal protection was increased to a total of 7in. of armor, with 8in. over the magazines. *Mississippi* was a member of the three-ship New Mexico class and carried a main battery of 12 14in guns. This class received the most modernization between the wars and thus had the best underwater protection of the USN's old battleships. Though at the time this was the most advanced underwater protection system fitted on any battleship, it would have been inadequate against a Japanese Type 93 torpedo. The oldest USN battleship present at Surigao Strait was *Pennsylvania*, launched in 1916. From October 1942 to February 1943, *Pennsylvania* underwent a refit and modernization that greatly increased her antiaircraft fit, but it did not address her underwater protection, which remained deficient.

USN battleships possessed a huge advantage over their IJN counterparts in the form of superior fire control systems. Each USN battleship carried a variety of radars, including fire control radar to augment its optical rangefinders. The Mark 8 radar was capable of blind fire (important in night combat) and could track a battleship-sized

Tennessee was rebuilt after Pearl Harbor. This view from July 1945 shows her configuration during the Battle of Surigao Strait. Note the triple 14in. gun turrets and the dual 5in./38 dual-purpose mounts. The Mk 34 main battery directors are clearly visible as is the Mk 8 radar fitted on top of them.

California's reconstruction was identical to Tennessee's and gave the ship state-of-the-art fire control and antiaircraft capabilities. The ship is painted in a striking dazzle camouflage pattern, which was the favored scheme for all three rebuilt battleships entering service in 1944.

target at 40,000 yards and smaller targets up to 31,000 yards. The three rebuilt battleships (*West Virginia*, *California*, and *Tennessee*) carried the Mark 8. The other three battleships carried the older and less capable Mark 3 fire control radar for their main batteries. It could provide range on a large target from 15,000 to 30,000 yards, but it lacked the beam definition to distinguish between the target and nearby shell splashes.

Cruisers

Three Treaty heavy cruisers were assigned to the Seventh Fleet. All carried a main battery of nine 8in. guns, but unlike their Japanese counterparts, no torpedoes. Early in the war, all Treaty cruisers demonstrated vulnerability to torpedo damage. The Australian *Shropshire* was a Royal Navy County-class heavy cruiser designed to treaty limitations. She was transferred to the Royal Australian Navy (RAN) in 1942 after the loss of her sister ship *Canberra*. She carried a main battery of eight 8in. guns and was even less well protected than USN Treaty cruisers.

The four light cruisers at Surigao Strait were powerful ships. Two Brooklyn-class ships (*Boise* and *Phoenix*) were better protected than heavy

Heavy cruiser *Louisville* was Oldendorf's flagship at Surigao Strait. The Treaty cruiser lacked the firepower protection of comparable IJN heavy cruisers.

Several Cleveland-class light cruisers fought during the battle. This is *Denver* in May 1944 following an overhaul. The ship's main battery of four triple 6in. gun turrets is visible as is her extensive antiaircraft and electronic suites.

cruisers of the period and carried a formidable main battery of 15 6in./47 guns, each capable of pumping out as many as 12 rounds per minute. The two Cleveland-class ships (*Columbia* and *Denver*) carried a main battery of 12 6in. guns, but in addition mounted a secondary battery of 12 5in./38 dual-purpose guns capable of firing as many as 20 rounds per minute. All ships carried modern fire control radars for antisurface and antiaircraft work.

Destroyers

A large number of Fletcher-class destroyers were available to Kinkaid and Oldendorf. Heavily armed, as indicated above, these ships had become proven ship-killers during the later stages of the Solomons campaign by virtue of the combination of the Mark 15 torpedo and radar. The problems associated with the Mark 15 had been addressed by late 1943, and when used correctly and allowed to mount radar-directed torpedo attacks, American destroyers proved themselves to be very capable surface warfare ships.

Killen was one of 175 Fletcher-class fleet destroyers commissioned by the USN during the war. These ships were heavily armed with five 5in./38 guns and ten torpedo tubes. *Killen* was one of several destroyers to hit *Yamashiro* with a Mark 15 torpedo and its 825lb warhead during the Battle of Surigao Strait.

Light carrier *Chitose* under attack by TF 58 aircraft, June 20, 1944. Converted from a seaplane carrier, she was unprotected but was a useful addition to the IJN's carrier force with an aircraft capacity of 30 aircraft. On October 25, she became one of only three aircraft carriers during the entire war to be sunk by surface ships.

IMPERIAL JAPANESE NAVY

The carrier force

Known as the Main Body, the IJN's carrier force was a shadow of its former self in October 1944. On paper, it looked formidable, with eight aircraft carriers and two converted battleships capable of carrying attack aircraft. In reality, it was a force with almost no striking power. The first two ships of the Unryu-class (*Unryu* and *Amagi*) comprised Carrier Division 1, but neither was fully operational. Carrier Division 3 included fleet carrier *Zuikaku* and three light carriers. Before the advent of the USN's Essex class, the two ships of the Shokaku class (*Shokaku* and *Zuikaku*) were the finest carriers in the world, with their mix of striking power (an air group of 75 aircraft), protection, speed, and range. Only *Zuikaku* remained after *Shokaku*'s loss at the Battle of the Philippine Sea. The light carriers included the veteran *Zuiho* and the newer *Chitose* and *Chiyoda*. All were converted from auxiliaries and were capable of embarking 30 aircraft. Though they had a decent top speed, they possessed no protection.

Carrier Division 4 was a mix of the converted carriers *Junyo* and *Ryuho* and the battleship-carriers *Ise* and *Hyuga*. No aircraft were available for the two converted carriers, so neither took part in *Sho-1*. The two battleships were part of the IJN's efforts to rebuild its carrier force in the aftermath of the defeat at Midway. Among the steps taken was the conversion of the two Ise-class battleships into hybrid battleship-carriers. This was accomplished by removing the two aft 14in. gun turrets and replacing them with a hangar and a 230ft-long flight deck. This deck was not capable of launching or landing aircraft. The 22 aircraft that could be embarked (a mix of conventional and float planes) were launched from two catapults. After launching, they recovered on other carriers or land bases. However, this awkward conversion was not worth the time and resources devoted to it. The ships never embarked

Ise in August 1943, after conversion into a hybrid carrier-battleship. Note the small deck aft that replaced the two aft 14in. turrets. The resources devoted to this conversion were totally wasted, since *Ise* and sistership *Hyuga* never carried a single aircraft into battle. At Leyte Gulf, they fought as conventional battleships.

This overhead view of an Akizuki-class destroyer shows the IJN's largest destroyer design of the war. The four twin 3.9in. mounts are visible as is the quadruple torpedo mount amidships. Four of these ships were assigned to escort Ozawa's carriers at Leyte Gulf and only two survived the battle.

aircraft in combat and the whole scheme was impractical. They were the slowest ships in Ozawa's force at 25 knots, but still remained useful, since they retained eight 14in. guns and a very heavy antiaircraft suite.

Ozawa's six heavy ships were allocated an escort of three light cruisers and eight destroyers. *Oyodo* was the newest of the light cruisers. Designed as a flagship for submarine flotillas, she had until recently been Toyoda's flagship. The 8,534-ton ship carried a main battery of six 6in./50 guns and was lightly protected. The other two cruisers, *Isuzu* and *Tama*, dated from 1921 to 1923 and were designed as destroyer flotilla leaders. They were in no way comparable to USN light cruisers. *Isuzu* had undergone conversion to an antiaircraft cruiser and carried six 5in. dual-purpose guns and 50 25mm guns.

The IJN designed large destroyers maximized to provide antiaircraft screening for carriers. This was the Akizuki class, four of which were assigned to Ozawa's force. It was the first IJN destroyer to embark the excellent Type 98 3.9in. gun that possessed a better range than the standard USN destroyer 5in./38 gun. Akizuki-class ships also carried four torpedo tubes filled with the excellent Type 93 torpedo and four reloads. Filling out the Main Body was a group of four Matsu-class destroyers. This was an austere design meant to be built in sufficient numbers to replace war losses. It carried only three 5in. guns and four torpedoes.

IJN carrier air groups
Two almost-trained carrier air groups were committed to the battle off Formosa

IJN Matsu-class destroyers were mass-produced to replace war losses. This image shows a Matsu-class unit (foreground) firing at American aircraft planes as the destroyer screens a carrier in the background during the Battle off Cape Engaño.

Yamashiro and *Haruna* in the late 1930s. *Yamashiro* is on the left and her profile reveals her distinctive pagoda-style forward superstructure. When launched in 1915, *Yamashiro* was one of the most powerful battleships afloat with a main battery of 12 14in. guns, but the lack of an extensive modernization between the wars meant that by 1944 she was a second-line unit.

Heavy cruiser *Nachi* survived the action in Surigao Strait and was sent to Manila after the battle. This view shows Shima's flagship under attack from aircraft from TG 38.3 in Manila Bay on November 5, 1944. The cruiser was sunk in this attack.

and suffered heavy losses. Since it was imperative that Ozawa's carriers had to embark some aircraft to enhance their fidelity as decoys, Toyoda ordered that the 653rd Air Group, which had not been transferred to Formosa, and whatever carrier-ready aircraft from the 601st Air Group assigned to Carrier Division 1 that were available be transferred to Carrier Division 3. This was quickly accomplished on October 19 and 20. This measure provided Ozawa with a total of 116 aircraft. Of these, 65 were embarked on *Zuikaku* (28 A6M5 Zero fighters, 16 A6M fighter-bombers, 7 D4Y2 "Judy" reconnaissance aircraft, and 14 B6N2 "Jill" torpedo bombers). The balance, 51 aircraft of which all were probably Zero fighters or fighter-bombers, was embarked on the three light carriers. The average standard of training for the pilots of these aircraft was extremely low.

Nishimura's force

The ships comprising Nishimura's small fleet were decidedly second rate. Battleships *Fuso* and *Yamashiro* were viewed as expendable, as shown by the serious consideration of a plan to send them to Saipan on a one-way mission to reinforce the garrison after the American invasion of the island. They possessed minimal combat power as the least modernized battleships in the IJN and were too slow to keep up with Kurita's main force. The fact they were sent into battle with an inadequate screen confirms that they were viewed as expendable. *Fuso* had spent much of 1943 and 1944 in the forward area, but she saw no action. *Yamashiro* was designated as a training ship for midshipmen in September 1943 and was not brought back to front-line status until the following September. Both ships possessed weak protection, particularly against torpedoes.

The rest of Nishimura's force was also second rate. *Mogami* was converted to an aircraft-carrying cruiser in 1943 and had lost two of her 8in. turrets. However, she was well protected and retained a battery of 12 torpedo tubes plus reloads. Nishimura's four destroyers were *Shiratsuyu* and three Asashio-class ships, the oldest assigned to Kurita's First Diversion Attack Force. Each carried eight torpedo tubes and eight reloads. None of

Fuso, shown here in 1934 with *Nagato* in the background, was also viewed by the IJN as a second-line unit by virtue of her slow speed and weak protection. This lack of protection was demonstrated at Surigao Strait when the ship sank after only two torpedo hits. There are several ways to tell the sisterships apart. *Fuso*'s pagoda superstructure had a different shape, her Number 3 14in. gun turret faced forward (not aft as on *Fuso*), and her aircraft-handling facilities were placed on top of turret Number 3.

Nishimura's ships had worked together, and their commanding officers were unknown to each other.

Table 3: Characteristics of the IJN ships at Surigao Strait

Ship	Tonnage (full load)	Principal weapons	Armor	Top speed
Battleships				
Fuso, Yamashiro	39,154	12 14in./45, 14 6in./50, 8 5in./40 DP	main belt 12in., horizontal 5.1in.	24.75 knots
Heavy cruisers				
Nachi, Ashigara	15,933	10 8in./50, 8 5in./40 DP, 16 24in. torpedo tubes	main belt 4in., horizontal 3in.	33 knots
Mogami	15,057	6 8in./50, 8 5in./40 DP, 12 24in. torpedo tubes	main belt 3.9in., horizontal 2.95in.	35 knots
Light cruisers				
Abukuma	7,094	5 5.5in., 2 5in./40 DP, 8 24in. torpedo tubes	main belt 2.36in., horizontal .78in.	35 knots
Destroyers				
Fubuki class (2)	2,050	4 5in./50, 9 24in. torpedo tubes	none	38 knots
Shiratsuyu class (1)	1,802	4 5in./50, 8 24in. torpedo tubes	none	34 knots
Asashio class (3)	2,370	4 5in./50, 8 24in. torpedo tubes	none	35 knots
Kagero class (2)	2,490	4 5in./50, 8 24in. torpedo tubes	none	35 knots

Shima's force

The seven ships making up Shima's force were grandiloquently named the Fifth Fleet, and then the Second Diversion Attack Force. The centerpiece of the force was its two heavy cruisers, which were fast, heavily armed, and crewed by well-trained men. Light cruiser *Abukuma* had been modernized before the war to carry two quadruple torpedo mounts with the Type 93 torpedo. This amazing weapon possessed a maximum range of 43,746 yards with a 1,082lb warhead. Each of Shima's destroyers carried eight or nine torpedo tubes filled with more Type 93s, with reloads.

IJN antiaircraft capabilities

How the IJN's surface forces fared in the face of intensive air attack was a key aspect of the battle. On October 24, the First Diversion Attack Force was subjected to over 250 USN offensive sorties. The following day, the Main Body was victim of more than twice as many. The First Diversion Attack Force was not neutralized, however, because super battleship *Musashi* acted as a torpedo and bomb sponge, leaving the rest of Kurita's force relatively unscathed. Ozawa's force fared much worse, losing four carriers in a single day, the only time in naval history such a loss was recorded. As the Japanese carriers could mount only a handful of CAP sorties, defense of the Main Body was left to its antiaircraft guns.

This pre-war view shows heavy cruiser *Ashigara*, one of four Myoko-class heavy cruisers involved in the battle. *Ashigara* survived the Battle of Surigao Strait, but she was sunk in June 1945 by a Royal Navy submarine.

The most common antiaircraft weapon on IJN surface combatants was the Type 96 25mm gun, which came in single, twin, and triple mounts. Knowing that it would have to operate under heavy enemy air attack, the IJN made great efforts to increase the antiaircraft fits of its combatants. For example, in the Main Body, *Ise* and *Hyuga* each carried 104 25mm guns, *Zuikaku* 96, and the light carriers between 68 and 46. Even light cruiser *Isuzu* carried 50 and the Akizuki-class destroyers almost 40. Unfortunately for the Japanese, the Type 96 25mm gun was a mediocre weapon. Its limitations, inadequate training and elevation speeds, low sustained rate of fire, and

Japanese naval forces came under an unprecedented level of air attack on October 24/25. Unfortunately for the IJN, their primary antiaircraft weapon was the Type 96 25mm gun, like these triple mounts on submarine *I-400* after the war. The Type 96 was a flawed weapon that offered only weak protection from air attack and took a low toll of American aircraft.

excessive blast that affected accuracy, were even recognized by the Japanese. In spite of the volumes of fire directed at American aircraft, their losses were continually light. While the 25mm gun was the IJN's stalwart antiaircraft weapon, it was augmented by the Type 89 5in. high-angle gun. This was a reliable weapon with high elevating speeds, a high muzzle velocity, and a large shell. Despite its good qualities, the weapon was inadequate because of its inferior fire control system, which was unable to track high-speed targets. The inadequacies of IJN antiaircraft weapons and their fire control systems meant Japanese surface ships were vulnerable to American air attack.

ORDERS OF BATTLE

UNITED STATES NAVY

THIRD FLEET

Admiral William F. Halsey aboard *New Jersey*.
Organization and strengths as of October 23, 1944

Task Force 38 (Vice Admiral Marc A. Mitscher aboard *Lexington*)
Task Group 38.1 (Vice Admiral John S. McCain aboard *Wasp*)

Carriers:

Hancock	Air Group 7
VB-7 (Bombing Squadron)	42 SB2C-3/3E
VF-7 (Fighter Squadron)	37 F6F-5, 4 F6F-5N
VT-7 (Torpedo Squadron)	18 TBM-1C
Hornet	Air Group 11
VB-11	25 SB2C-3
VF-11	40 F6F-3/3N/3P/5/5N/5P
VT-11	18 TBM/TBF-1C
Wasp	Air Group 14
1 F6F-3	
VB-14	10 F6F-3/5, 25 SB2C-3
VF-14	42 F6F-3/3N/3P/5/5N
VT-14	18 TBM/TBF-1C/1D

Light carriers:

Monterey	Air Group 28
VF-28	23 F6F-5/5P
VT-28	9 TBM-1C
Cowpens	Air Group 22
VF-22	26 F6F-5/5P
VT-22	9 TBM-1C

Screen:
Heavy cruisers *Chester*, *Pensacola*, *Salt Lake City*
Destroyers *Bell*, *Boyd*, *Brown*, *Burns*, *Caperton*, *Case*, *Cassin*, *Charrette*, *Cogswell*, *Conner*, *Cowell*, *Cummings*, *Downes*, *Dunlap*, *Fanning*, *Grayson*, *Ingersoll*, *Izard*, *Knapp*, *McCalla*, *Woodworth*

Task Group 38.2 (Rear Admiral Gerald R. Bogan aboard *Intrepid*)

Carrier:

Intrepid	Air Group 18
1 F6F-5	
VB-18	28 SB2C-3
VF-18	43 F6F-3N/5/5P
VT-18	18 TBM-1C

Light carriers:

Cabot	Air Group 29
VF-29	21 F6F-3/5
VT-29	9 TBF/TBM-1C
Independence	Night Air Group 41
VFN-41	19 F6F-3/5/5N
VTN-41	8 TBM-1D

Screen:
Battleships *Iowa*, *New Jersey*
Light cruisers *Biloxi*, *Miami*, *Vincennes*
Destroyers *Benham*, *Colahan*, *Cushing*, *Halsey Powell*, *Hickox*, *Hunt*, *Lewis Hancock*, *Marshall*, *Miller*, *Owen*, *Stephen Potter*, *Stockham*, *The Sullivans*, *Tingey*, *Twining*, *Uhlmann*, *Wedderburn*, *Yarnell*

Task Group 38.3 (Rear Admiral Frederick C. Sherman aboard *Essex*)

Carriers:

Essex	Air Group 15
1 F6F-3	
VB-15	25 SB2C-3
VF-15	50 F6F-3/3N/3P/5/5N
VT-15	20 TBF/TBM-1C
Lexington	Air Group 19
1 F6F-3	
VB-19	30 SB2C-3
VF-19	41 F6F-3/3N/3P/5/5N/5P
VT-19	18 TBM-1C

Light carriers:

Langley	Air Group 44
VF-44	25 F6F-3/5
VT-44	9 TBM-1C
Princeton	Air Group 27
VF-27	25 F6F-3/5
VT-27	9 TBM-1C

Screen:
Battleships *Massachusetts*, *South Dakota*
Light cruisers *Birmingham*, *Mobile*, *Reno*, *Santa Fe*
Destroyers *Callaghan*, *Cassin Young*, *Clarence K. Bronson*, *Cotton*, *Dortch*, *Gatling*, *Healy*, *Porterfield*, *Preston*

Task Group 38.4 (Rear Admiral Ralph E. Davison aboard *Franklin*)

Carriers:

Enterprise	Air Group 20
1 F6F-5	
VB-20	34 SB2C-3
VF-20	39 F6F-3N/5
VT-20	19 TBM-1C
Franklin	Air Group 13
1 F6F-5	
VB-13	31 SB2C-3
VF-13	38 F6F-3/3N/5/5N/5P
VT-13	18 TBM/TBF-1C

Light carriers:

Belleau Wood	Air Group 21
VF-21	25 F6F-3/5
VT-21	7 TBM-1C
San Jacinto	Air Group 51
VF-51	25 F6F-5/5P
VT-51	9 TBM-1C

Screen:
Battleships *Alabama, Washington*
Heavy cruisers *New Orleans, Wichita*
Destroyers *Bagley, Gridley, Helm, Irwin, Laws, Longshaw, Maury, McCall, Morrison, Mugford, Nicholson, Patterson, Prichett, Ralph Talbot, Swanson, Wilkes*

Task Force 34 (formed October 25, 1944)
Battleships *Alabama, Iowa, Massachusetts, New Jersey, South Dakota, Washington*
Heavy cruisers *New Orleans, Wichita*
Light cruisers *Biloxi, Miami, Mobile, Santa Fe, Vincennes*
Destroyers *Bagley, Caperton, Clarence E. Bronson, Cogswell, Cotton, Dortch, Healy, Hickox, Hunt, Ingersoll, Knapp, Lewis Hancock, Marshall, Miller, Owen, The Sullivans, Tingey*

Task Group 34.5 (formed October 25, 1944)
Battleships *Iowa, New Jersey*
Light cruisers *Biloxi, Miami, Vincennes*
Destroyers *Hickox, Hunt, Lewis Hancock, Marshall, Miller, Owen, The Sullivans, Tingey*

Cruiser–destroyer Group formed October 25 under Rear Admiral DuBose to pursue remnants of Main Body
Heavy cruisers *New Orleans, Wichita*
Light cruisers *Mobile, Santa Fe*
Destroyers *Bagley, Callaghan, Caperton, Clarence K. Bronson, Cogswell, Cotton, Dortch, Healy, Ingersoll, Knapp, Patterson, Porterfield*

Pacific Fleet-supporting submarines
Task Force 17 (Vice Admiral Charles A. Lockwood)
Atule, Barbel, Besugo, Blackfish, Drum, Gabilan, Jallao, Haddock, Halibut, Icefish, Pintado, Ronquil, Salmon, Sawfish, Seadragon, Shark, Silversides, Snook, Sterlet, Tang, Trigger, Tuna

SEVENTH FLEET

Task Group 77.2 (Rear Admiral Oldendorf aboard *Louisville*)
Battle Line (Rear Admiral Weyler aboard *Mississippi*)
Battleship Division 2
    Battleships *California, Pennsylvania, Tennessee*
Battleship Division 3
    Battleship *Mississippi*
Battleship Division 4
    Battleships *Maryland, West Virginia*
Destroyer Division X-ray (Commander Hubbard)
    Destroyers *Aulick, Claxton, Cony, Sigourney, Thorn, Welles*
Left Flank Force (Oldendorf)
Cruiser Division 4 (Oldendorf)
    Heavy cruisers *Louisville, Minneapolis, Portland*
Cruiser Division 12 (Rear Admiral Hayler)
    Light cruisers *Columbia, Denver*
Destroyer Squadron 56 (Captain Smoot)
    Destroyer Division 111 (Smoot)
        Destroyers *Bennion, Heywood L. Edwards, Leutze, Newcomb, Richard P. Leary*
    Destroyer Division 112 (Captain Conley)
        Destroyers *Albert W. Grant, Bryant, Halford, Robinson*
Right Flank Force (Rear Admiral Berkey aboard *Phoenix*)
Cruiser Division 15 (Berkey)
    Heavy cruiser HMAS *Shropshire*
    Light cruisers *Boise, Phoenix*
Destroyer Squadron 24 (Captain McManes)
    Destroyers HMAS *Arunta, Bache, Beale, Daly, Hutchins, Killen*
Special Attack Force (Captain Coward aboard *Remey*)
Destroyer Squadron 54 (Coward)
    Destroyer Division 107 (Coward)
        Destroyers *Monssen, Remey*
    Destroyer Division 108 (Commander Phillips)
        Destroyers *McDermut, McGowan, Melvin*
Task Group 70.1 Motor Torpedo Boat Squadrons, Seventh Fleet (Commander Bowling)
Surigao Strait Patrols (Lieutenant Commander Leeson)
    Section 1: *PT-130, PT-131, PT-152*
    Section 2: *PT-127, PT-128, PT-129*

Section 3: *PT-146, PT-151, PT-190*
Section 4: *PT-191, PT-192, PT-195*
Section 5: *PT-150, PT-194, PT-196*
Section 6: *PT-132, PT-134, PT-137*
Section 7: *PT-324, PT-494, PT-497*
Section 8: *PT-523, PT-524, PT-526*
Section 9: *PT-490, PT-491, PT-493*
Section 10: *PT-489, PT-492, PT-495*
Section 11: *PT-321, PT-326, PT-327*
Section 12: *PT-320, PT-330, PT-331*
Section 13: *PT-323, PT-328, PT-329*

IMPERIAL JAPANESE NAVY

MAIN BODY

Vice Admiral Ozawa aboard *Zuikaku*
Carrier Division 3 (Ozawa)
Fleet carrier *Zuikaku*
Light carriers *Chitose, Chiyoda, Zuiho*
Air Groups 653 and 601 with a total strength of 80 A6M5 "Zero" fighters and fighter-bombers, 25 B6N2 "Jill" torpedo-bombers, 4 B5N2 "Kate", 7 D4Y "Judy" dive-bombers
Carrier Division 4 (Rear Admiral Matsuda)
Battleship-carriers *Hyuga, Ise* (neither ship embarked any aircraft)
Light cruisers *Oyodo, Tama*
Torpedo Squadron 61
Destroyers *Akizuki, Hatsuzuki, Wakatsuki*, plus *Shimotsuki* from Torpedo Squadron 41
Escort Squadron 31
Light cruiser *Isuzu*
Torpedo Squadron 43
    Destroyers *Kiri, Kuwa, Maki, Sugi*
Supply Unit
Destroyer *Akikaze*
Escort ships *CD-22, CD-29, CD-33, CD-43, CD-132*
Oilers *Jinei Maru, Takane Maru*

FIRST DIVERSION ATTACK FORCE, THIRD SECTION

Vice Admiral Nishimura aboard *Yamashiro*
2nd *Sentai*
Battleships *Fuso, Yamashiro*
Heavy cruiser *Mogami*
Torpedo Division 4
Destroyers *Asagumo, Michishio, Shigure, Yamagumo*

SECOND DIVERSION ATTACK FORCE

Vice Admiral Shima aboard *Nachi*
16th *Sentai*
Heavy cruisers *Ashigara, Nachi*
1st Torpedo Flotilla
Light cruiser *Abukuma*
7th Torpedo Division
    Destroyers *Akebono, Ushio*
18th Torpedo Division
    Destroyers *Kasumi, Shiranuhi*
21st Torpedo Division
    Destroyers *Hatsushimo, Hatsuharu, Wakaba*

SOUTHWEST AREA FLEET GUARD FORCE

Vice Admiral Sakonju aboard *Aoba*
16th *Sentai*
Heavy cruiser *Aoba*
Light cruiser *Kinu*
Destroyer *Uranami*

OPPOSING PLANS

THE AMERICAN PLAN

The Philippines occupy a critical geostrategic location in Southeast Asia. In particular, Luzon dominates the sea lines of communication (SLOCs) to and from the South China Sea. American control of that SLOC threatened Japan with economic strangulation and jeopardized its ability to continue the war. Gaining a toehold on Leyte was the first step to seizing Luzon.

Leyte was selected as the location for the first invasion in the Philippines for several important reasons. It offered an undefended approach from the Philippine Sea. Leyte Gulf offered a large anchorage and was therefore suitable as a staging point for future operations. Airfields on Leyte could project fighter coverage to central Luzon, the Visayas in the central Philippines, and the southern part of Mindanao. The central location of Leyte and its control of Surigao Strait offered an excellent jumping-off point for follow-on operations into the Visayas and beyond.

Since Leyte was over 500 miles from the nearest American airfield, carrier aircraft would have to supply air cover for the invasion. MacArthur believed that the entire operation hinged on the ability of the USN to keep the Japanese from attacking the invasion force or reinforcement and resupply convoys while denying the movement of Japanese reinforcements to Leyte.

The only American naval force capable of defending the invasion shipping from strong Japanese attacks and of stopping significant Japanese reinforcement of Leyte was the Third Fleet. The Seventh Fleet, part of MacArthur's Southwest Area Command, was capable of defending the invasion force from local Japanese attacks.

Kinkaid's operation plan assumed that the IJN would mount a major operation to defeat the landing. This worst-case scenario planning was in contrast to the intelligence assessment that stated that such a major Japanese reaction was unlikely. The Third Fleet had a major role in Kinkaid's plans, which included striking Japanese airfields up until D-Day (October 20) and then operating in strategic support by carrying out additional strikes as the situation dictated.

Nimitz's operation plan was in congruence with MacArthur's in almost all respects. The Third Fleet was tasked to support the invasion by destroying Japanese air and naval forces in Formosa and throughout the Philippines. However, there was one important difference in Nimitz's directive to Halsey. Buried in a subparagraph was the emphasis given to Halsey stating, "in case opportunity for destruction of major portion of the enemy fleet offers or can be created, such destruction becomes the primary task." This was a blank check for Halsey to place destruction of the Japanese fleet above passive operations to protect the invasion force, even though this new task from Nimitz did not replace the original task of providing cover and support to the invasion forces.

Halsey's operation order issued on October 4 directed that TF 38 would concentrate off Samar after refueling on October 19 to support the landings the following day in coordination with the Seventh Fleet. His orders emphasized that Third Fleet units should attack Japanese forces within range and that TF 34 should play a large role in offensive operations. Halsey believed the need to cooperate with the Seventh Fleet should not discourage offensive operations by his command.

There were two major problems with American planning before the battle. Firstly, top commanders did not believe that the IJN would make a major effort to contest the landings. This belief was based on an assessment of Japanese intentions, rather than their capabilities. The result was a slow reaction when the scope of the Japanese response became apparent. Secondly, and most importantly, the divided command structure posed problems for intelligence, logistics, air searches, and submarine deployments. The lack of an overall commander made the situation for naval forces much more complicated. The Third Fleet was not under MacArthur's command, and its commander was given orders by Nimitz that diverged from MacArthur's intent. This left much room for interpretation by Halsey and was to play a major part in the upcoming battle.

THE JAPANESE PLAN

To defend Japan's final defensive perimeter, the Imperial General Headquarters developed four plans covering any likely area that might come under American attack. *Sho-1* covered the Philippines, which was considered the Americans' most probable next target. Planning the naval component of *Sho-1* was the responsibility of the Combined Fleet under Admiral Toyoda. He fully bought into the notion that the IJN had no choice but to defend the Philippines. If the Philippines were lost, and Japan lost access to the resources of Southeast Asia, then the fleet would become "a white elephant" in his view. Toyoda admitted after the war that the plan he had devised was contrary to accepted wisdom, but he felt he had no choice but to commit the remaining strength of the Combined Fleet before it became irrelevant.

Among the many handicaps that Toyoda had to deal with was the fact that in the aftermath of the disastrous Battle of the Philippine Sea the remaining strength of the Combined Fleet was geographically divided. This was a severe handicap, since the preferred plan was to employ the Combined Fleet as one force and because the division was severe—the two parts of the fleet were some 2,500NM apart. This separation was driven by fuel considerations. The carriers had to remain in Japan to train new aviators, while the bulk of the surface fleet had to return to Lingga Roads near Singapore to be near available fuel supplies. There were inadequate fuel reserves in Japan to maintain the entire fleet there.

Toyoda issued specific instruction for the employment of the Combined Fleet during the first five days in August. The basic plan remained in place until the battle commenced, but details were changed as the situation demanded. The primary objective was to destroy the American invasion landing force before it could disembark troops and equipment. This required the First Diversionary Attack Force to hit the invasion force within two days of it arriving off Leyte. To enable the First Diversion Attack Force to penetrate to the enemy's landing site, the Main Body and the Second Diversionary Attack Force, supported by land-based aircraft, were tasked to attack and neutralize the American carrier force. In early September, the plan underwent an important modification. The new version called for the Main Body and the Second Diversionary Attack Force to draw the American carrier force to the north. Ozawa further modified this variant by trimming the Main Body from the original eight carriers to only four, since this was enough to act as a lure.

Timing was key for *Sho-1* to succeed. This proved a problem from the start. By October 17, the various forces slated to participate in the operation had been alerted. The original timeline had Kurita storming into Leyte Gulf at dawn on the 22nd. To support this movement, Ozawa's Main Body had to depart Japan on the 19th and successfully draw TF 38 to the north sometime on the 21st. Speed was of the essence since the American landing occurred on the 20th, and with each passing day the hope for crippling the invasion receded.

Kurita informed Toyoda that he would depart Lingga at 0100hrs on October 18 and arrive at Brunei on the 20th. However, the tankers he needed to refuel from would not arrive at Brunei until the 21st. This made the planned October 22 arrival at Leyte Gulf impossible. If Kurita's force departed Brunei on the 22nd after refueling, it would not arrive off Leyte until the 24th. The need to refuel the destroyers on the way made this unlikely; the 25th was the final date set by Kurita for the attack into the gulf. Ozawa also had problems adhering to the original schedule. Because of the need to load aircraft, he could not leave the Inland Sea until the afternoon of the 20th.

The plan for the main attack by Kurita's force was changed on the eve of battle. On the morning of the 20th, Kurita received a message from the Combined Fleet that it assessed that the attack into Leyte Gulf would be better conducted as a pincer attack instead of as a single penetration. It was not a direct order to change the plan, but in typical Japanese style it was worded as a preference. As this was not a suggestion that Kurita could refuse, it was adopted and was the origin of the Battle of Surigao Strait. The main force under Kurita was still slated to enter Leyte Gulf from the north, but the new wrinkle had a smaller force coming into the gulf from the south through Surigao Strait.

Changing the plans at this late point in proceedings and inserting Shima's Second Diversion Attack Force into the mix (see below) was counterproductive. The final plan had to be set before the conference on Kurita's flagship in Brunei Bay at 1700hrs on October 21. By the time the conference began, Kurita decided to detach his two oldest battleships and build a small force under the command of Vice Admiral Nishimura to carry out the southern penetration into Leyte Gulf. This force was routed into the Sulu Sea, then the Mindanao Sea, and was scheduled to arrive in Leyte Gulf at dawn on the 25th.

It is important to examine the timelines for the entry of Kurita's and Nishimura's forces into the gulf. The original timeline had Nishimura arriving off the beachhead at 0430hrs and Kurita's main force at 0600hrs. Kurita was content to leave this alone, since this set up Nishimura's force as a diversion before the arrival of the main force. Conjecture that Nishimura's force was nothing more than a sacrificial decoy is further supported by the fact that it was so small that it could be nothing else. This is almost certainly how Nishimura viewed his role and explains why he was so intent on maintaining his schedule. Some of the participants in the operation also saw this as the case and one of the crewmen on *Fuso* recalled being briefed that the mission was a "surface special attack."

The planning for Shima's small force was emblematic of the shambolic state of IJN organization for the battle. His force was originally assigned to Ozawa as part of the Main Body. Then it was detached to go down to Formosa to mop-up Halsey's Third Fleet in the aftermath of the Battle off Formosa. Then it was assigned to the Southwest Area Fleet based in Manila to spearhead an envisioned counter-landing on Leyte. The commander of the Southwest Area Fleet, Vice Admiral Mikawa, determined that the Shima force was not required to accomplish the counter-landing mission. On October 19 Toyoda rejected this and instructed Mikawa to use the Shima force as part of the counter-landing force. In spite of this and after confirming that the counter-landing operation did not require Shima's force, Mikawa sent orders to Shima on the afternoon of the 19th that he was not required to stand by to support the counter-landing.

Shima was already planning how to use his force to support the attack into Leyte Gulf, since he considered the transport mission was unsuitable. When Mikawa cut him loose from the counter-landing, Shima was quick to propose a plan that his force cooperate with Kurita's force to storm into Leyte Gulf on October 25. The details of the operation were significant. The attack would be through Surigao Strait and would be conducted independently but in cooperation with Kurita. At this point, it is unclear if Shima was aware of the Combined Fleet's suggestion that Kurita conduct a pincer attack into Leyte Gulf.

Early afternoon on October 21, the Combined Fleet again ordered Shima to take part in the transport mission and ordered his force to Manila. At this point, two forces were assigned to the counter-landing operation with a total of five cruisers and eight destroyers. This was a very questionable use of the Combined Fleet's limited resources. Mikawa kept at it and badgered Combined Fleet headquarters twice on the 21st to release Shima's force for combat duties. Finally, Toyoda relented on the morning of the 22nd. The Shima force was released to cooperate with Kurita's force in the attack into Leyte Gulf.

It needs to be kept in mind that as Mikawa and Tokyo debated how to use Shima's force, Nishimura's force had already received orders to use Surigao Strait for its attack into Leyte Gulf. Kurita was unaware that Shima's force would also be released to take the same approach. The only authority aware of this was the Combined Fleet and it made no attempt to coordinate the operations of the two forces.

When finally released, Shima's plan was to follow up Nishimura's attack by some five hours, arriving at the area of the American beachhead at 0900hrs on October 25. This delay was seen as appropriate by Toyoda, who did not micro-manage his field commanders. As the battle developed, Shima increased speed to be only about an hour behind Nishimura, but it was never his intent, nor that of Toyoda or Kurita, that he more closely coordinate or possibly integrate the two forces coming through Surigao Strait.

Assessment of Operation *Sho-1*

The objective of Toyoda's plan, to hit the invasion force before it could disembark its troops, was impossible with *Sho-1*. Because the exact timing of the American invasion was unknown (in large measure because of a lack of reconnaissance from land-based aircraft) and given the distance that the First Diversion Attack Force had to cover from its base near Singapore, the earliest the IJN could attack the landing force was five days after it arrived off Leyte. This delay meant that *Sho-1* could never destroy the invasion force or stop the landing. The clever diversionary aspect to the plan was forced on Toyoda and was simply another indication of the basic weakness of *Sho-1*.

If everything went according to plan, Kurita's force would arrive at Leyte Gulf five days after the initial American landings and have the opportunity to attack empty transports, if any remained there at all. Kurita and his staff saw this clearly and advocated another modification to the basic plan that would allow the fleet's primary objective to shift to fighting the American carrier fleet if it came within striking distance. This would be a much better use of the IJN's remaining surface strength instead of a pointless death attacking empty transports.

Aside from the incorrect objective of the *Sho-1* plan, there were other problems impairing its execution. The biggest one was the disparity in strength between the IJN and the USN in October 1944. *Sho-1* contained the dubious premise that surface forces could operate without air cover and move significant distances under air attack and still achieve their objectives. Another serious problem glossed over by Toyoda was the high level of coordination required from forces spread over a wide area. The intricate nature of *Sho-1* was typical of IJN operational planning, and just as it had during every other major IJN operation of the war, *Sho-1* experienced severe communication and coordination issues that threw the entire plan into turmoil. The fact that *Sho-1* did not contain any method to neutralize the Third Fleet, only to temporarily divert it, meant that even if Kurita's force had succeeded in reaching Leyte Gulf it would have been caught in the gap between the Seventh and Third Fleets and likely annihilated. Examined objectively, *Sho-1* had no chance of reversing the course of the war and had a much higher chance of bringing on the complete destruction of the Combined Fleet. It provided the IJN with a glorious opportunity to go down fighting, thus defending the IJN's peculiar brand of honor, than a possibility to affect the outcome of the war.

Track of IJN Forces, October 15–25, 1944

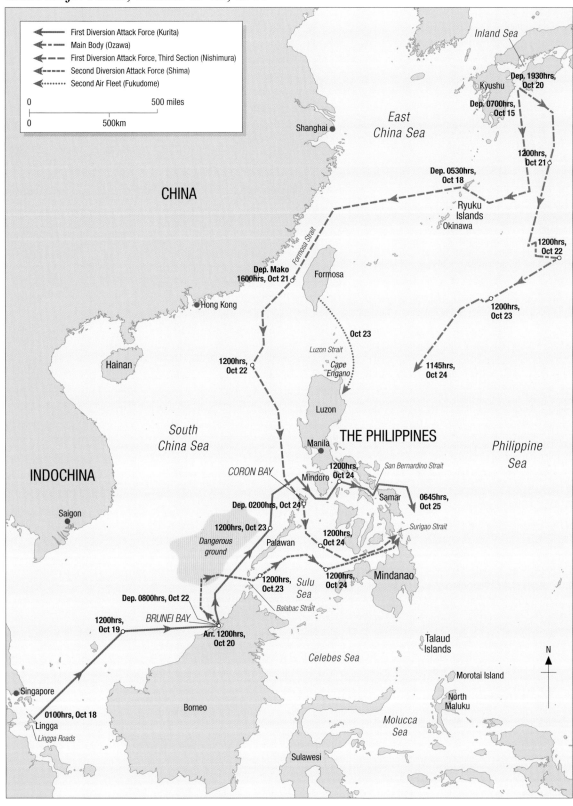

Legend:
- First Diversion Attack Force (Kurita)
- Main Body (Ozawa)
- First Diversion Attack Force, Third Section (Nishimura)
- Second Diversion Attack Force (Shima)
- Second Air Fleet (Fukudome)

0 — 500 miles
0 — 500km

Inland Sea

Kyushu

Dep. 1930hrs, Oct 20

Dep. 0700hrs, Oct 15

East China Sea

Shanghai

1200hrs, Oct 21

CHINA

Dep. 0530hrs, Oct 18

Ryuku Islands

Okinawa

1200hrs, Oct 22

Formosa Strait

Dep. Mako 1600hrs, Oct 21

Formosa

1200hrs, Oct 23

Hong Kong

Hainan

Oct 23

Luzon Strait

Cape Engano

1145hrs, Oct 24

1200hrs, Oct 22

Luzon

South China Sea

THE PHILIPPINES

Manila

Philippine Sea

INDOCHINA

San Bernardino Strait

CORON BAY

Mindoro

1200hrs, Oct 24

Saigon

Dep. 0200hrs, Oct 24

Samar

0645hrs, Oct 25

1200hrs, Oct 23

Dangerous ground

Palawan

1200hrs, Oct 24

Surigao Strait

Mindanao

1200hrs, Oct 23

Sulu Sea

1200hrs, Oct 24

Dep. 0800hrs, Oct 22

Balabac Strait

1200hrs, Oct 19

BRUNEI BAY

Talaud Islands

Arr. 1200hrs, Oct 20

Celebes Sea

N

Morotai Island

Singapore

North Maluku

Borneo

0100hrs, Oct 18

Lingga

Lingga Roads

Molucca Sea

Sulawesi

THE BATTLE

SHO-1 BEGINS

The American invasion of Leyte began at 1000hrs on October 20. At two different locations, a corps of two divisions landed against sporadic opposition on the eastern side of Leyte. The first hours of an amphibious operation are always the most precarious. Despite this obvious vulnerability, only weak air attacks were mounted by land-based Japanese aircraft against the huge invasion force; the nearest IJN force could not threaten the beachhead for another five days.

A lack of intelligence on the exact timing of the American invasion meant that Toyoda had to confirm that the American invasion was underway before he committed the Combined Fleet. When Japanese observers on Suluan Island in the eastern approaches to Leyte Gulf reported the approach of American naval forces on October 17, Toyoda ordered all *Sho-1* forces on alert. Kurita's First Diversion Attack Force was ordered to Brunei. This huge force departed Lingga just after midnight on the 18th. A small force of heavy cruiser *Aoba*, light cruiser *Kinu*, and destroyer *Uranami* detached from Kurita's main force and headed for Manila to take part in the counter-landing operation.

Toyoda issued the execute order for *Sho-1* at 1110hrs on October 18. Though the need for speed was paramount, the soonest Kurita's force could reach Leyte Gulf was the morning of the 25th. This was the fatal flaw in *Sho-1*. By October 25, there would be no invasion shipping in the gulf to attack, and the invasion force with 132,400 men and just under 200,000 tons of supplies was firmly ashore. The initial American assault ships quickly unloaded and departed by the evening of October 20. The first reinforcement group arrived on the 22nd, unloaded, and departed the same day. The second reinforcement group, comprising 33 tank landing ships (LST), 24 Liberty ships, and ten support ships, arrived on the 24th. At midnight on the same day, shipping inside Leyte Gulf totaled three amphibious flagships, one assault transport, 23 LSTs, two medium landing ships, and 28 Liberty ships.

When the First Diversion Attack Force arrived at Brunei Bay to refuel, Kurita called a conference of his principal officers. For the first time, they learned the details of *Sho-1*. Many officers present were appalled that the fleet was being committed to attack empty transports and doubted that the plan offered any prospect for success. Kurita and every other senior officer were savvy enough to realize that the plan's success was a long shot, but

The American landing on Leyte went off smoothly on October 20. Here light cruiser *Boise* conducts a bombardment in support of the landing force.

Kurita reminded those present of the "glorious opportunity" they had been given. His final words "Would it not be a shame to have the fleet remain intact while the nation perishes? What man can say that there is no chance for our fleet to turn the tide of war in a decisive battle?" reflected the doubts in his mind but roused all present to do their best.

The bulk of the First Diversion Attack Force departed Brunei at 0800hrs on October 22 and headed northeast through the Palawan Passage. Nishimura's Third Section delayed its departure until 1500hrs. Once it departed, Nishimura's small force headed to Balabac Strait and then into the Sulu Sea. If all went to plan, the two parts of the First Diversion Attack Force would be reunited inside Leyte Gulf during the early hours of October 25.

OPERATIONS ON OCTOBER 24

For the Japanese, October 24 was a crucial day. This was the day on which they had planned to deal with Halsey's Third Fleet, either by diversion or direct attack, while their surface forces would move toward Leyte Gulf. For the Americans, it became clear by October 23 that the IJN was making a major effort to disrupt the invasion. Halsey's carriers had their hands full the next day repelling attacks from land and even carrier-based aircraft while launching the heaviest attacks on a naval force yet seen in the war.

The critical element of *Sho-1* was the neutralization of the Third Fleet. The most direct way to do this was to attack it. On the morning of October 24, TG 38.3 with its four carriers was located east of Luzon by Japanese land-based aircraft. In an all-out effort, over 200 sorties were flown against it throughout that day. Some of these never found a target, and many that did get near TG 38.3 were intercepted by defending Hellcats. One Japanese dive-bomber escaped interception and made a skillful attack against light carrier *Princeton*. A single 551lb bomb penetrated the flight deck and set fire to six fully armed and fully fueled Avengers. The flames spread quickly, and the crew was ordered off the ship at 1010hrs, except for those personnel fighting the fires. Spreading flames eventually reached the torpedo magazine resulting in a huge explosion at 1523hrs. Since the ship could not be towed to safety, it was ordered to be scuttled. *Princeton* was the first USN fast carrier sunk since October 1942, but the attack fell far short of neutralizing TF 38.

The inability to put Halsey's carriers out of action by direct attack, and the failure of Ozawa to perform his diversion mission during the day (see below), meant that TF 38 was free to deliver a series of strikes against the First Diversion Attack Force. The Americans flew a total of 252 sorties in five separate attacks against Kurita's force as it steamed through the Sibuyan Sea without air cover. Super battleship *Musashi* was sunk and a heavy cruiser damaged, which was forced to return to Singapore. Other ships were

Track of TF 38 and the Main Body, October 24, 1944

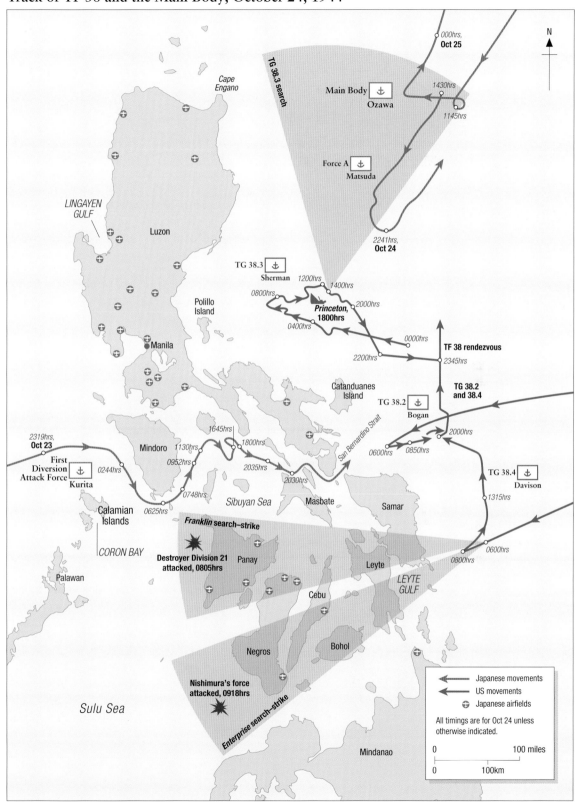

N

000hrs, **Oct 25**

1430hrs

Main Body
Ozawa

1145hrs

TG 38.3 search

Cape Engano

Force A
Matsuda

2241hrs, **Oct 24**

LINGAYEN GULF

Luzon

TG 38.3
Sherman

1200hrs   *1400hrs*

0800hrs   *2000hrs*

Polillo Island

0400hrs

Princeton, **1800hrs**

0000hrs

Manila

2200hrs

TF 38 rendezvous
2345hrs

Catanduanes Island

TG 38.2
Bogan

TG 38.2 and 38.4

2000hrs

San Bernardino Strait

0600hrs   *0850hrs*

2319hrs, **Oct 23**

First Diversion Attack Force
Kurita

0244hrs

Mindoro   *1130hrs*   *1800hrs*

0952hrs

1645hrs

2035hrs

0748hrs   *2030hrs*

0625hrs

Calamian Islands

Sibuyan Sea

Masbate

Samar

TG 38.4
Davison

1315hrs

0600hrs

CORON BAY

Franklin search–strike

Destroyer Division 21 attacked, 0805hrs

Panay

Leyte

0800hrs

LEYTE GULF

Palawan

Cebu

Negros   Bohol

Nishimura's force attacked, 0918hrs

Sulu Sea

Enterprise search–strike

Mindanao

←	Japanese movements
←	US movements
⊕	Japanese airfields

All timings are for Oct 24 unless otherwise indicated.

0   100 miles

0   100km

damaged, but Kurita retained a force of four battleships, six heavy and two light cruisers, and 11 destroyers. After briefly turning back in the afternoon to seek relief from the unrelenting air attacks, Kurita headed back to the east at 1714hrs toward San Bernardino Strait en route to Leyte Gulf.

While focusing on the much larger Kurita force, TF 38 also directed sorties at Nishimura's force. The seven ships making up Nishimura's force departed Brunei Bay at 1500hrs on October 22 and headed for the Sulu Sea by Balabac Strait. Nishimura knew that if he could gain the element of surprise then his chances of success would be greatly improved. However, if the Americans spotted Nishimura's force, they could set up an ambush in Surigao Strait.

In fact, there was little chance Nishimura's force could have approached Leyte Gulf undetected. Of TF 38's three task groups, TG 38.4 was operating the farthest south. Under command of Rear Admiral Davison, it included fleet carriers *Enterprise* and *Franklin* and light carriers *Belleau Wood* and *San Jacinto*. These launched a reinforced search mission at 0600hrs to search the Sulu Sea. Under perfect weather conditions, 32 Hellcats and 24 Avengers headed west.

Enterprise's air group covered the southern part of the Sulu Sea. At 0855hrs, radar on *Yamashiro* detected the approaching American aircraft, ending any hope Nishimura had of getting to Surigao Strait undetected. A total of 28 *Enterprise* aircraft were airborne organized into two search groups each with six Avengers (each with two 500lb bombs instead of torpedoes) and eight Hellcats. The initial contact report issued by the *Enterprise* search group gave the exact composition of Nishimura's force—two Fuso-class battleships, one Mogami-class cruiser, and four destroyers. The commander of the group that spotted the Japanese ships waited for the arrival of the second group to allow for a coordinated attack.

Each of the two groups attacked one of Nishimura's battleships. Against *Yamashiro*, the Avengers were only able to gain a near miss on the starboard side that opened some plates and caused a brief list. The battleship was heavily strafed by Hellcats, which caused the death of 20 men. Damage to *Fuso* was more extensive. A direct hit was recorded beside Number 2 14in. turret, but it caused little damage. A second bomb struck the fantail by the aircraft catapult. Nearby aviation fuel caught fire, destroying both float planes and creating thick black smoke. The situation seemed serious, but 25 minutes after the American aircraft had departed, the fire was out, and *Fuso* was able to proceed with the rest of the force.

During the 20-minute ordeal, *Mogami* was also attacked, but she suffered only minor damage. Operating to the west of Nishimura was Shima's Second Diversion Attack Force and also in the area was Shima's detached Destroyer Division 21 with three ships, which was hurrying to rejoin Shima's main force after having completed a transport mission to Manila.

Toyoda's massive air attacks planned for October 24 against TF 38 were only partially successful. Light carrier *Princeton* was hit by a single bomb and incurred fatal damage. This is the carrier burning, but still underway, about 20 minutes after she was hit.

Franklin's air group was assigned the northern sector of the Sulu Sea. It spotted the three ships of Shima's Destroyer Division 21 off Panay. Attacking high-speed destroyers was a challenge for any airman, but at 0813hrs *Wakaba* was hit by a bomb and several near misses. The damage proved fatal—45 minutes later, *Wakaba* sank with the loss of 30 men. *Franklin* launched a follow-up strike of 12 Hellcats and 11 bombers that reached the two remaining destroyers just before noon. Only one bomb hit was scored against *Hatsushimo*, which did little damage. The Japanese commander decided to head back to Manila with the survivors of *Wakaba*. Inexplicably, he failed to notify Shima of his decision. Destroyer Division 21 was out of the battle.

TG 38.4 was ordered to move north to join the attack on Kurita's force in the Sibuyan Sea at 1024hrs. This saved Nishimura from further air attacks. Shima's main force was not attacked on October 24, but it was spotted by long-range aircraft around noon. By the time the report reached Kinkaid at 1435hrs, it was interpreted as another sighting of Nishimura's force. American aircraft spotted all three Japanese forces operating in the Sulu Sea on October 24, but failed to develop an accurate picture of their overall strength.

THE BATTLE OF SURIGAO STRAIT

Of the four major engagements comprising the Battle of Leyte Gulf, the Battle of Surigao Strait was clearly the least important. As far as the Japanese were concerned, it was a diversionary attack mounted by a small group of ships judged to be the least capable in the First Diversionary Attack Force. Nevertheless, the clash in Surigao Strait has taken on greater historical importance than it otherwise deserves, because it was the last ever battleship duel. During the entire Pacific War, IJN and USN battleships clashed only twice. The first was during the climactic Japanese push to retake Guadalcanal in November 1942 when battleship *Kirishima* was pitted against the much more modern and capable *South Dakota* and *Washington*. In spite of the fact that this was a night engagement and *Kirishima* was being escorted by a large number of torpedo-armed cruisers and destroyers while the

American battleships had only a patchwork escort of four destroyers, the battle ended badly for the Japanese. *Washington* used radar-guided gunnery to sink *Kirishima* and suffered no damage in return. *South Dakota* suffered extensive topside damage but was in no danger of sinking. When the second and last battleship clash of the Pacific War occurred in Surigao Strait, the result was the same as the first.

The Americans prepare

The detection of Nishimura's force on October 24 gave Kinkaid ample time to prepare. The assessment of the Japanese forces headed toward him was two battleships (and some reason was given to believe four), four heavy and four light cruisers, and ten destroyers, which was much greater than the combined strength of Nishimura's and Shima's forces. It was unclear if there were two or three different groups of Japanese ships. For Kinkaid, a doubt remained as to whether the Japanese were going to attempt to force the strait or if they were just escorting a troop convoy. He ordered Rear Admiral Oldendorf to defend the northern neck of Surigao Strait as the Japanese could attempt to force the strait on the night of October 24/25.

Oldendorf began his preparations during the afternoon of the 24th, and he drafted the battle plans personally. All movement by remaining shipping inside the gulf was stopped at sunset. He orchestrated a set-piece battle that virtually eliminated any prospect that some portion of Nishimura's force could slip into the gulf. Oldendorf's objective was the protection of the transports at all costs. He decided to position his battle line under Rear Admiral Weyler off Hingatungan Point in the northern portion of the strait, because it offered the maximum sea room available while still restricting Japanese movements. He considered it possible that the Japanese might try to slip light forces into the gulf to the east of Hibuson Island (located in the middle of the strait) during the battle-line engagement, so he stationed most of his destroyers on the left flank.

Eight cruisers were divided into two groups and placed 2.5NM south of the battle line. Oldendorf commanded the left flank cruiser group with three heavy and two light cruisers; Rear Admiral Berkey commanded the Right Flank unit comprised of one heavy and two light cruisers. Another valuable light cruiser, *Nashville*, had to remain off the beachhead out of harm's way because its passenger, General MacArthur, refused to leave the ship and join Kinkaid on his flagship. Twenty-four destroyers were arrayed to screen the battleships and cruisers, and on both flanks well south of the heavy ships in position to launch torpedo attacks on the approaching Japanese. The right flank destroyers were ordered to attack first, followed by the left flank ships. By using radar to execute their torpedo attacks, it was expected that considerable

PT-131 prepares for battle on October 24 as the Japanese approach Surigao Strait. The principal weapons of these boats were its four Mark 8 torpedoes, which are visible in this image. This weapon had a maximum range of 16,000 yards and a top speed of 36 knots. Despite the limitations of the Mark 8, PT boats succeeded in hitting two Japanese ships during the battle.

attrition could be inflicted on the Japanese. In the southern approaches to the strait and into the Mindanao Sea, 39 patrol torpedo boats (PT) were deployed to give ample warning of Japanese movements and to make torpedo attacks when possible.

During the afternoon, Oldendorf summoned Weyler and Berkey to his flagship, heavy cruiser *Louisville*, to review the plan. Nothing was left to chance. Later in the evening, another five destroyers were added to the mix when Captain J.G. Coward submitted a plan to Oldendorf to have his ships take part in torpedo attacks. Never

before had the USN been able to plan a night battle so carefully and with such overwhelming force.

However, there was one major concern for the Americans. The heavy ships had been loaded with a predominate mix of high explosive shells, instead of armor piercing, in expectation of bombarding Yap, later changed to Leyte. Against the battleships known to be included in the Japanese force, high explosive rounds would be ineffective. To make the available armor-piercing shells count, it was decided that the battleships would only open fire after the Japanese closed to between 17,000 and 20,000 yards.

The action between Nishimura's force as it transited Surigao Strait and Kinkaid's PT boats resulted in few casualties, but it did give the Americans ample warning of Nishimura's approach. This is damage suffered by *PT-152*.

The approach phase

The first units to encounter Nishimura's force were the PT boats operating in the Mindanao Sea. The 39 boats were divided into 13 sections, each with three boats. They were ordered to first report all contacts, attack independently when the situation allowed, and then clear the area when American destroyers and cruisers showed up. In the dark, the PT boats awaited the Japanese while remaining stationary in their patrol areas so as to make no wake and to create the best conditions for using their radar.

Little is known about Nishimura's precise thinking as he approached the strait. He was planning on arriving off Tacloban at 0430hrs on October 25 in accordance with Toyoda's master plan that had Kurita's force arriving off Leyte a short time later. This schedule fell apart after Kurita's advance was thrown off schedule on the afternoon of October 24 when he temporarily turned around in the face of intensive air attack in the Sibuyan Sea. At 2013hrs Nishimura sent a message to Toyoda and Kurita that he planned to arrive off Dulag at 0400hrs the next morning, a half hour later than planned. This was only a minor change; much more important was the receipt at 2200hrs of Kurita's message that he would not be in the gulf until 1100hrs. This meant that Nishimura's force was on its own when it executed its attack into the gulf. However, Nishimura did not change his plan after learning of Kurita's revised intentions. He was determined to force the strait in darkness and in so doing draw forces away from Kurita's main attack.

Nishimura divided his force up as it approached Surigao Strait. *Mogami* and three destroyers were sent ahead to investigate, followed by the two battleships and destroyer *Shigure*. The battle began at 2236hrs when *PT-131* gained radar contact on Nishimura's main force. The three boats of the section headed toward the contact to make a torpedo attack. Two of the

Surigao Strait: Attack of Destroyer Squadron 54, October 25, 1944

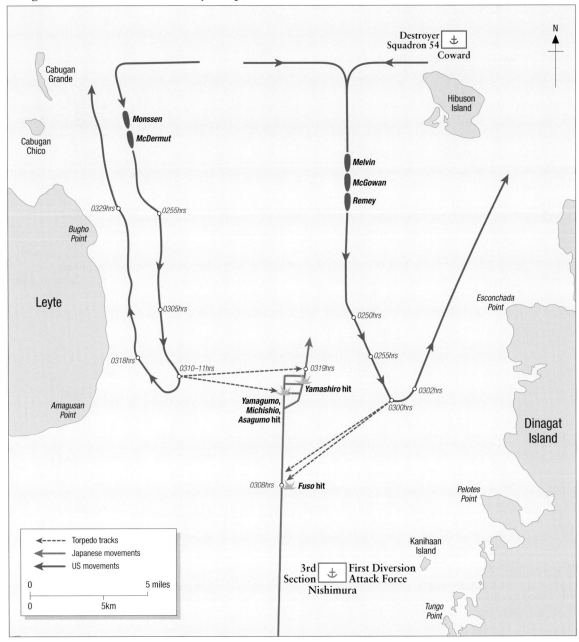

boats were slightly damaged, but one was able to close within torpedo range. News of the contact did not reach Oldendorf until 0026hrs on October 25. Another section sighted the advance group built around *Mogami* at 2350hrs and two of the boats fired a torpedo at the cruiser. Neither hit its target. Demonstrating the confusion in any night battle, at about 0100hrs *Mogami* was hit by a 6in. shell from *Fuso*. Though a dud, it killed three men. About an hour later, *PT-134* closed to within 3,000 yards of *Fuso* and fired three torpedoes. Again, all missed. This running series of encounters continued up until 0213hrs. Of the 39 boats, 30 contacted the Japanese and launched

34 torpedoes. None of Nishimura's ships was hit. While Nishimura's force was successfully fighting its way up the strait in good order, he kept Kurita and Shima informed of his progress. At 0040hrs, the two parts of Nishimura's force reunited. First blood went to the Japanese, since ten PTs were hit, and one (*PT-493*) sank, with a total of three dead and 20 wounded. Though unable to exact any attrition on the Japanese, the PTs had provided an invaluable service informing Oldendorf of Nishimura's location and strength.

Destroyer *McDermut* launched the deadliest USN torpedo salvo of the war. This salvo accounted for three Japanese destroyers sunk or damaged. The Japanese totally underestimated the capabilities of USN destroyers executing radar-guided torpedo attacks and paid the price.

Melvin was the Fletcher-class destroyer which fired the torpedoes that sank battleship *Fuso*. This is the ship's scoreboard, which includes a profile of the Japanese battleship.

Based on an earlier report from one of *Mogami*'s scout aircraft on the location and numbers of USN ships in Leyte Gulf, Nishimura appeared to believe that the battle would occur inside Leyte Gulf and not in Surigao Strait. If he really believed that Oldendorf would not use favorable geography to his advantage, he was sorely mistaken. Having survived the PT boat attacks with no damage, Nishimura now faced a much more deadly threat. This came in the form of five Fletcher-class destroyers under the command of the aggressive Coward. Two other destroyers from Coward's Destroyer Squadron 54 were left on picket duty and did not take part in the torpedo attack. The five destroyers assigned to the attack were arrayed to conduct an anvil attack (with torpedoes coming in from both bows of the enemy target), with *McDermut* and *Monssen* from the west and *Remey*, *McGowan*, and *Melvin* from the east. Approaching at 30 knots, Coward's ships would launch torpedoes guided by radar, and refrain from using their 5in. guns so as not to give their positions away. Once the torpedoes were on their way, the destroyers would break off and head north along the coast to clear the area and reduce the possibility of a friendly fire incident. What ensued was one of the most successful attacks of the entire war.

The first radar contact from the eastern group of destroyers was made at 0240hrs. Contact by the western group followed at 0254hrs. Though spotted by *Shigure*, the American destroyers were able to maneuver into ideal firing positions. Even as the Americans drew near, Nishimura failed to order any evasive maneuvers against possible torpedo attack. Just after 0300hrs, Coward's three destroyers fired 27 torpedoes from between 8,200 to 9,300 yards at the approaching Japanese. After releasing their weapons, the Americans came under ineffective fire but were able to disengage with no damage. At 0308hrs, two torpedoes launched from *Melvin* hit *Fuso*.

The two destroyers steaming to the west of Nishimura's force were also able to develop an excellent firing solution. Against ineffective defensive fire, the two ships launched a full salvo of 20 torpedoes at 0310–0311hrs. Against this latest barrage, Nishimura ordered a change of course that brought his screen into danger. Beginning at 0319hrs, the

USN DESTROYERS TORPEDO BATTLESHIP *FUSO* (PP.48–49)

The only Japanese battleship sunk by surface torpedo attack during the Pacific War was *Fuso* at Surigao Strait. The instrument of her destruction was Destroyer Squadron 54 with its five Fletcher-class destroyers. These ships were deployed in two sections, an eastern group with *Remey*, *McGowan*, and *Melvin* and a western group with *McDermut* and *Monssen*. The eastern group was the first to gain radar contact on Nishimura's force at 0240hrs. Radar contact from the western group followed at 0254hrs. Captain J.G. Coward, commander of Destroyer Squadron 54, planned to subject the approaching Japanese to an anvil attack with the ten torpedoes carried aboard each of his ships. Though the anvil attack did not come off as planned, the attack was a brilliant success, primarily because Nishimura failed to order evasive maneuvers before the torpedoes reached their targets. Throughout the action, the Japanese failed to appreciate the threat from American destroyers, while their optical and electronic sensors failed to give warning of impending attack. Coward's three destroyers in his eastern group fired 27 torpedoes from between 8,200 to 9,300 yards just after 0300hrs. Only after releasing their weapons did the USN destroyers come under ineffective Japanese shellfire, but none of the American ships was hit.

This view shows the destroyers *McGowan* (**1**) and *Remey* (**2**) firing their torpedoes and turning away with 6in. shells from *Yamashiro* bursting around them (**3**). *Yamashiro* (**4**) can be seen in the background with her searchlights attempting to locate the American destroyers. Minutes later, at 0308hrs, two torpedoes from *Melvin* hit *Fuso*. The battleship fell out of line and later sank with the loss of almost her entire crew.

American torpedoes began to strike their targets. Three from *McDermut* hit *Yamagumo*, which blew up and sank in two minutes with the loss of all but two of her crew. Another *McDermut* torpedo hit *Michishio* amidships and flooded both engine rooms. The destroyer came to a stop, and according to her commanding officer (one of only four survivors) the ship sank in 15 minutes. The final blow from *McDermut*'s deadly salvo was against *Asagumo*. A single torpedo hit her bow, which broke off, reducing her speed to 13–15 knots. Three other torpedoes passed just ahead of *Shigure*. *McDermut*'s ten torpedoes were the most effective salvo of the war from any American destroyer.

The other destroyer from the western group, *Monssen*, also scored. One of her torpedoes hit *Yamashiro* on her port quarter. The damage did not impair her speed, but the ship's captain ordered the magazines to the two rear 14in. turrets flooded as a precaution. This reduced her firepower by a third. Nishimura reported the loss of two of his destroyers and the damage to *Yamashiro* to Kurita and Shima at 0330hrs. He was unaware of the full extent of the disaster inflicted by American torpedoes. Damage to *Fuso* from her two torpedo hits proved fatal. One torpedo found its mark forward abreast the forward 14in. gun turret and the second hit aft, which flooded one of the boiler rooms and caused a fire. Unbeknown to Nishimura, *Fuso* soon fell out of line and headed south. According to her few survivors, the battleship sank by the bow at about 0345hrs. Their accounts contradict the generally accepted version that the torpedoes blew *Fuso* into two parts with each remaining afloat. *Fuso*'s destruction was another disaster for the IJN; of her crew of 1,630 officers and men, only ten returned to Japan.

Coward's torpedo attack was brilliantly executed and extremely devastating. All but two of Nishimura's seven ships were hit. Three sank soon after being torpedoed, and the other was forced out of the battle.

When the next torpedo attack developed, only *Yamashiro*, *Mogami*, and *Shigure* remained operational. Destroyer Squadron 24 included five Fletcher-class destroyers and the Royal Australian Navy Tribal-class destroyer *Arunta*. The six destroyers were split into two groups of three and approached Nishimura's force from the west along the coast of Leyte. The first group began its attack at 0323hrs firing a total of 14 torpedoes from between 6,500 and 6,800 yards. Only one found a target. At about 0331hrs, a torpedo from *Killen* hit *Yamashiro* amidships on her port side that temporarily reduced her speed to 5 knots. The second group of destroyers fired a total of 15 torpedoes between 0329hrs and 0336hrs. Destroyer *Bache* opened fire with her 5in. guns and *Yamashiro* replied with her secondary battery. None of the torpedoes found a target and the gunfire from both sides was also ineffective. Before clearing the area, the destroyers exchanged gunfire with *Yamashiro*, *Mogami*, and probably *Asagumo*. None of the American ships was damaged.

Before the beginning of the climactic gunnery phase, one more group of American destroyers conducted a torpedo attack. This was Destroyer Squadron 56 from the left flank of Oldendorf's formation. Nine destroyers deployed in three sections of three approached Nishimura's reduced column on both bows. The first two sections, attacking from both bows, fired a half-salvo of five torpedoes from each destroyer, but none found a target. Gunfire from the Japanese ships was similarly ineffective. The final section came in from dead ahead of the Japanese ships and closed to within 6,200 yards before launching 13 torpedoes. One of these, either from *Albert*

Surigao Strait: Attack of Destroyer Squadrons 24 and 56, October 26, 1944

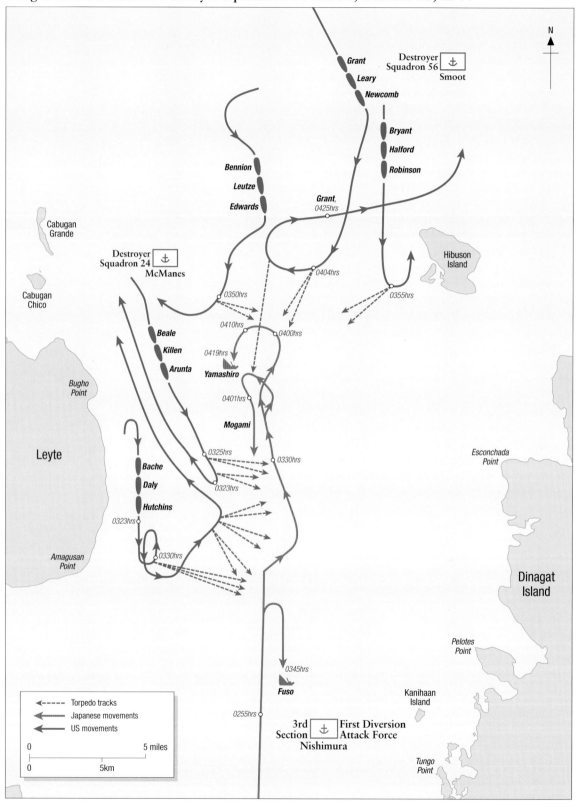

N

Grant

Leary

Newcomb

Destroyer
Squadron 56
Smoot

Bryant

Halford

Robinson

Bennion

Leutze

Edwards

Grant,
0425hrs

Cabugan
Grande

Hibuson
Island

Destroyer
Squadron 24
McManes

Cabugan
Chico

0404hrs

0350hrs

0355hrs

Beale

Killen

Arunta

0410hrs

0400hrs

0419hrs

Yamashiro

Bugho
Point

Esconchada
Point

0401hrs

Mogami

Leyte

0325hrs

0330hrs

Bache

Daly

0323hrs

Hutchins

0323hrs

Dinagat
Island

0330hrs

Amagusan
Point

Pelotes
Point

0345hrs

Fuso

Kanihaan
Island

0255hrs

3rd
Section
Nishimura

First Diversion
Attack Force

Tungo
Point

◄-----	Torpedo tracks
◄─────	Japanese movements
◄─────	US movements

0   5 miles

0   5km

52

W. Grant or *Bennion*, hit *Yamashiro* in her starboard engine room at 0407hrs. Two torpedoes from *Newcomb* hit the battleship at 0411hrs, also on her starboard side.

By the time the final group of destroyers broke off to head north out of the area, the gunnery duel between Oldendorf's heavy ships and Nishimura's remaining ships was in full swing. Positioned between both forces, they came under fire from both the American cruisers and the Japanese. The rearmost destroyer, *Albert W. Grant*, was hit by the first of 18 shells at 0407hrs. Eleven of the hits were made by 6in. shells from *Denver* with the other seven coming from the Japanese. *Albert W. Grant* was pulled out of danger by another destroyer, but not before 34 of her crew were killed and another 94 wounded.

The only American ship damaged at Surigao Strait was destroyer *Albert W. Grant*, shown here in 1945 after repairs. The destroyer was caught in crossfire between American and Japanese forces and was hit by shells from both. Deconfliction of friendly forces during night battles was a severe challenge throughout the war.

The first phase of the battle had gone even better than Oldendorf could have hoped. In exchange for damage to one destroyer, Nishimura's force lost the bulk of its combat power. Only three Japanese ships remained to take on the American battle line. *Yamashiro* was able to shake off her initial torpedo damage and had restored 18 knots by 0337hrs. As he approached the northern part of the strait, Nishimura ordered his force to reduce speed to 12 knots.

The battleships clash

As Nishimura plodded bravely up the strait, his progress was being followed by radar aboard the American battleships and cruisers. First contact was gained at 0323hrs at a range of 33,000 yards. Every advantage was held by the Americans. In addition to overwhelming strength, they knew the location and strength of the enemy while Nishimura had no idea what he was up against. Tactically, the Americans gained the rarely achieved advantage of "capping the T." This meant the advancing Japanese could only fire their forward guns as the Americans could pound away with full broadsides.

Photos of night engagements are few and usually of poor quality. This view shows battleship *West Virginia* firing during the Battle of Surigao Strait. The photograph was taken from battleship *Pennsylvania*, which never fired her weapons during the engagement.

Admiral Weyler ordered the battleships to open fire at 26,000 yards (even though the Japanese were already closer than this) and Oldendorf held the cruisers' fire until the Japanese closed to 15,600 yards.

The gunnery battle began at 0351hrs when the first American cruiser opened up. Two minutes later, *West Virginia* commenced fire from 22,800 yards. All ships fired at the largest radar return of the three Japanese ships, which was *Yamashiro*. The American barrage grew as each battleship gained a fire control solution. The three ships with the most modern fire control systems did most of the work. *California* joined in at 0355hrs

This view, also taken from *Pennsylvania*, shows the gun flashes of USN cruisers during the Battle of Surigao Strait. Unless the cruisers continued to maneuver, they presented potential targets for Japanese torpedoes.

from 20,400 yards followed by *Tennessee* one minute later. The three battleships with the less capable Mk 3 fire control radar struggled to gain a firing solution. *Maryland* opened fire at 0359hrs by ranging her Mk 3 radar on the shell splashes from the other battleships. *Mississippi* took until 0412hrs when she fired a full salvo at *Yamashiro* from 19,790 yards. *Pennsylvania* never gained a good solution for her 14in. main battery and failed to fire a single salvo.

The cruisers added additional weight to the barrage directed at Nishimura's three ships. Initially, *Yamashiro* was the target at 0351hrs, but *Portland* later shifted fire to *Mogami* and *Denver* targeted a destroyer that turned out to be *Albert W. Grant*. The high rate of fire by the light cruisers made for high ammunition expenditures. The five left-flank cruisers fired a total of 3,100 6in. and 8in. shells. Of these, light cruiser *Columbia* accounted for an incredible 1,147. The right-flank cruisers fired 1,077 6in. and 8in. shells, despite *Shropshire*'s slowness to engage and to deliberate rate of fire.

During the 18-minute gunnery action, *Yamashiro* put up a brave fight in an utterly hopeless situation. Hundreds of 6in., 8in., 14in., and 16in. shells splashed around her. The first salvo from *West Virginia* hit *Yamashiro*'s forward superstructure. Nishimura was not wounded and remained on the bridge until the ship capsized. The number of actual hits will never be known, but by 0356hrs *Yamashiro* was observed to be burning amidships, aft and in her bridge area. Nevertheless, *Yamashiro* was able to maintain 12 knots and fired back with her two forward 14in. turrets. At 0356hrs she targeted *Phoenix*; at 0359hrs, *Columbia* was subjected to near misses. At 0401hrs, she straddled *Shropshire* with several salvos. *Denver* also reported coming under fire. However, no American ships were hit by 14in. shells. *Yamashiro*'s secondary battery blazed away at the American destroyers and almost certainly contributed to the damage suffered by *Albert W. Grant*.

As American gunfire ravaged *Yamashiro*'s topside, the final three torpedo hits on *Yamashiro*'s starboard side, from either *Albert W. Grant* or *Bennion* and *Newcomb*, constituted mortal damage. Oldendorf ordered a ceasefire at 0409hrs after it was apparent his destroyers were being subjected to "friendly" fire. *Yamashiro* turned south during this lull and increased speed to 14 knots. After the final two torpedo hits at 0411hrs, the battleship came to a stop and developed a severe list. Her captain ordered the crew to abandon ship. *Yamashiro*'s brave but futile fight came to an end at 0419hrs when she capsized to port. Only three survivors of the some 150 men in the water chose to be picked up by American ships. Of the 1,636 men aboard, only ten saw Japan again. Nishimura went down with his ship.

Heavy cruiser *Mogami* also took tremendous punishment before sinking. The cruiser had been heavily damaged in June 1942 at the Battle of Midway,

Surigao Strait: the gunnery phase

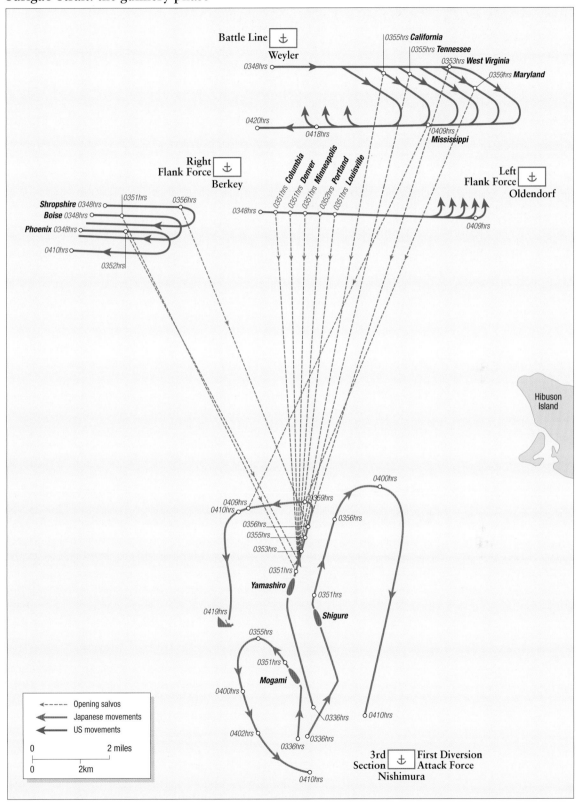

Battle Line ⚓ Weyler

0348hrs

0355hrs **California**
0355hrs **Tennessee**
0353hrs **West Virginia**
0359hrs **Maryland**

0420hrs
0418hrs
0409hrs
Mississippi

Right Flank Force ⚓ Berkey

Left Flank Force ⚓ Oldendorf

Columbia
Denver
Minneapolis
Portland
Louisville

0351hrs 0351hrs 0351hrs 0352hrs 0351hrs

Shropshire 0348hrs
0351hrs
0356hrs
Boise 0348hrs
Phoenix 0348hrs
0410hrs
0352hrs

0348hrs
0409hrs

Hibuson Island

0400hrs
0409hrs 0369hrs
0410hrs
0356hrs
0356hrs
0355hrs
0353hrs
0351hrs
0351hrs
Yamashiro
Shigure
0419hrs

0355hrs
0351hrs
Mogami
0400hrs
0336hrs
0410hrs
0402hrs
0336hrs
0336hrs
0410hrs

3rd Section ⚓ First Diversion Attack Force
Nishimura

Legend:
← - - - Opening salvos
← Japanese movements
← US movements

0 | 2 miles
0 | 2km

55

and on this occasion, she again proved to be a tough opponent. In the early phase of the battle, she took several 5in. hits from American destroyers. In the first minutes of the withering barrage from Oldendorf's cruisers and battleships, *Mogami* sustained more damage, including a hit on one of her 8in. turrets. After firing four Type 93 torpedoes at 0401hrs against the gun flashes from enemy ships to the north, she came under fire from heavy cruiser *Portland*. Two 8in. shells hit *Mogami*'s bridge at 0402hrs, killing her commanding officer, and other shells disabled two engine rooms. The new commanding officer decided to break off the action and head south at slow speed. While headed south, she encountered the Second Diversion Attack Force.

The sojourn of the Second Diversion Attack Force

The Fifth Fleet, the IJN force responsible for defense of the North Pacific, was designated the Second Diversion Attack Force for *Sho-1*. By August 1944, this small force had been pulled back to the Inland Sea for intensive training in preparation for the forthcoming decisive battle. It was placed under the command of Ozawa's Main Body.

Shima's force was almost drawn to an early destruction in the aftermath of the air–sea battle off Formosa. Reports of great destruction wrought by Japanese air attacks seemed to be supported by the detection of two American cruisers being towed out of the battle area. These were *Houston* and *Canberra*, which were torpedoed on October 13 and 14, respectively. Halsey hoped to use them to draw out portions of the Japanese fleet. The two cruisers and their light escort were given the informal designation "Cripple Division 1" and dangled before the Japanese. Two carrier task groups were positioned nearby to spring the trap if the Japanese took the bait.

After being ordered to be ready to steam on October 10, Shima's force of heavy cruisers *Nachi* and *Ashigara*, light cruiser *Abukuma*, and seven destroyers departed the Inland Sea through Bungo Strait and headed south in the early hours of October 15. The orders for Shima's small force were to mop up "cripples" from TF 38 and rescue downed Japanese aviators. Dispatching Shima's small force on such a mission was entirely quixotic and provided another example of the muddled thinking at the IJN's highest echelons during the battle. Whatever damage suffered by TF 38, it still dwarfed a force built around only two heavy cruisers operating with no air cover.

Japanese air searches on October 16 detected the virtually intact TF 38. This unfortunate truth was relayed to Shima when his ships came under attack that afternoon. Shima wisely decided to head north to get out of range and arrived at Amani-O-Shima on the afternoon of October 17. So far, Shima had been lucky. After exiting the Inland Sea, Shima's force was spotted by USN submarines on October 15 and then twice more on October 18 and again on October 20. None of the submarines was able to close for a torpedo attack. After stopping briefly at Amani-O-Shima, Shima departed the next morning for Mako in the Pescedore Islands (located between China and Formosa).

Yet another indication of the fatuous nature of IJN planning for the "decisive" battle of Leyte Gulf was the planning for and operation of the Second Diversion Attack Force. What to do with Shima's force appears to have been an afterthought. While on the way to Mako on October 18, Shima received orders detaching his command from Ozawa's Main Body and placing it under Admiral Mikawa's Southwest Area Fleet. Shima's force was directed to go to Manila where it would join with Cruiser Division 16 detached from Kurita's fleet. The combined force under Shima was slated to conduct a counter-landing operation on the western side of Leyte. Shima did not relish the opportunity of escorting troop transports when he thought he should be breaking into Leyte Gulf to destroy the American invasion fleet. He instantly started to devise his own plans to put his force into the fight. These were supported by Mikawa, who thought that the counter-landing mission could be accomplished without Shima's force.

As the debate continued on how to employ his force, Shima arrived at Mako on the morning of October 20. Toyoda ordered Shima's force to carry out its original mission of supporting the movement of troops from Manila to Leyte, crushing Shima's design of charging into Leyte Gulf. Mikawa refused to let the issue drop, and eventually Tokyo relented. Accordingly, Shima departed Mako at 1600hrs on October 21. Very early the next morning, submarine *Seadragon* sighted the force, which was identified as having a carrier. The submarine was able to close to within 3,000 yards of the supposed carrier to fire four torpedoes along the radar bearing, but the torpedoes missed. Several hours later, at about 0900hrs, another submarine spotted Shima's force but was too far away for a torpedo attack. Without further distraction, Shima arrived at Coron Bay to refuel at 1800hrs on October 23. Instead, no tankers were waiting for him, forcing Shima to refuel his destroyers from his two heavy cruisers. As his four remaining destroyers refueled, Shima received word from his three detached destroyers from Destroyer Division 21 that they had completed their transport mission to Manila and would rejoin him the next evening to take part in the attack into Leyte Gulf.

At 0200hrs on October 24, the Second Diversion Attack Force departed Coron and headed to Surigao Strait. As already mentioned, Shima's force was detected during the day as it transited the Sulu Sea, but it was not attacked.

However, the movement of Shima's force was not coordinated with Nishimura's. Shima designed his advance so he could attack separately from Nishimura's force. The gap between the forces was originally five hours, but Shima reduced this to two hours by the time his force began entering the strait. As he entered Surigao Strait on the night of October 24/25, Nishimura issued reports during the early part of his transit, which Shima received, but when he met serious resistance, the reports stopped. Shima was therefore unaware of the virtual annihilation of Nishimura's force. The only information available was gunfire flashes in the distance and snippets of radio traffic from Nishimura's ships under attack.

Oldendorf was aware that a second force was moving to support Nishimura. The first firm indication of this was a contact report from the PT boats on Shima's force at 0038hrs. Oldendorf knew he was dealing with two widely spaced Japanese forces. Just as Nishimura was forced to deal with incessant PT boat attacks, now it was Shima's turn. These turned out to be more than a mere nuisance. Shima's introduction to combat came at about 0315hrs when *PT-134* mounted an ineffective attack. Ten minutes later, disaster struck the Japanese. As Shima's force steamed off the southern tip of Panaon Island in the southern approaches to the strait, *PT-137* crept to within 900 yards of one of the Japanese destroyers and launched a torpedo attack. The torpedo passed underneath the destroyer, but then continued

Second Diversion Attack Force at Surigao Strait

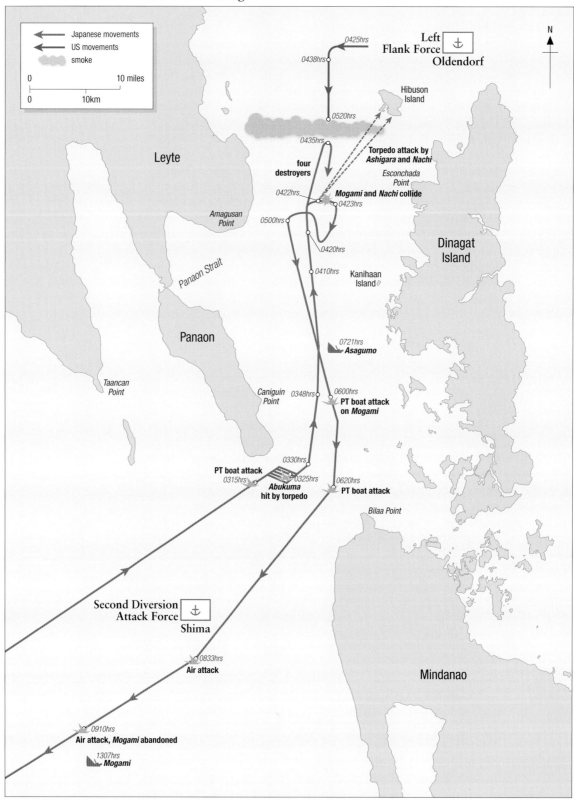

Japanese movements
US movements
smoke

0   10 miles
0   10km

0425hrs

Left
Flank Force
Oldendorf

0438hrs

Hibuson
Island

0520hrs

Leyte

0435hrs

four
destroyers

Torpedo attack by
Ashigara and *Nachi*

*Esconchada
Point*

0422hrs

Mogami and *Nachi* collide

0423hrs

0500hrs

Amagusan
Point

0420hrs

Dinagat
Island

0410hrs

Kanihaan
Island

Panaon Strait

0721hrs
Asagumo

Panaon

Taancan
Point

Caniguin
Point

0348hrs

0600hrs

PT boat attack
on *Mogami*

0330hrs

PT boat attack

0315hrs

0325hrs

Abukuma
hit by torpedo

0620hrs

PT boat attack

Bilaa Point

Second Diversion
Attack Force
Shima

0833hrs
Air attack

Mindanao

0910hrs
Air attack, *Mogami* abandoned

1307hrs
Mogami

58

toward light cruiser *Abukuma*. It struck the cruiser in its forward boiler room. The explosion killed 30 men, and reduced *Abukuma*'s speed to 10 knots, forcing her to leave Shima's formation.

Shima's remaining two cruisers and four destroyers increased speed to 28 knots. Shima was still oblivious of Nishimura's fate, but sighting ships on fire prompted him to believe that Nishimura's attempt to force the strait had not been successful. *Shigure* emerged out of the darkness and continued to head south at high speed. *Nachi*'s radar picked up contacts 13,000 yards away and Shima ordered his two cruisers and four destroyers to prepare for gun and torpedo action. Without Shima's approval, his chief of staff ordered the two cruisers to maneuver for a torpedo strike against the distant and indistinct radar contacts. At 0422hrs *Nachi* and *Ashigara* each fired eight Type 93 torpedoes at the radar contacts. In fact, these were Oldendorf's flagship *Louisville* followed by *Portland*. Despite the element of surprise, the Japanese torpedo attack completely failed.

Immediately after firing its torpedo broadside, *Nachi* faced disaster. The burning *Mogami* had loomed out of the darkness minutes before. *Nachi*'s skipper failed to grasp that *Mogami* was underway, not stationary, and he failed to take proper measures to avoid the damaged cruiser. As *Nachi* was unable to pass forward of *Mogami*, the two ships side-swiped each other forward at 0423hrs. Frantic last-second maneuvers lessened the impact of the collision, but the result was still dramatic. *Nachi* took the worst of it, suffering a large gash in her bow at the waterline on her port side. Damage to the bow reduced her speed to 18 knots.

Shima's four destroyers continued north but were unable to find a target. At 0435hrs, Shima gave them orders to break off and head south. As *Nachi* worked up to 18 knots, Shima contemplated his options. Senior officers on the bridge advised him to suspend the advance up the strait fearing they were only headed for certain destruction. Shima agreed, stating well after the war that his withdrawal was driven by his desire not to fall into a trap. Unable to gauge the enemy's strength, and having just had his flagship disabled, Shima's decision appears logical. He explained his thinking in a short message to Mikawa: "This force has concluded its attack and is retiring from the battle area to plan subsequent action." Just like Kurita would do several hours later, Shima declined the opportunity to suffer a pointless death.

The pursuit

Lost in this one-sided battle is the lack of an aggressive American pursuit that permitted Shima's force to escape without additional damage. At about the same time as *Nachi* was running into *Mogami*, Oldendorf was ordering his forces south to finish off the fleeing Japanese. The battleships were too valuable to risk in the darkness, so only the cruisers and destroyers were involved. *Denver*, one of the left-flank cruisers, reported three large contacts (the three IJN heavy cruisers) 14NM to the south. Oldendorf wanted his last six destroyers with a full torpedo load to lead the pursuit. These were formed into an improvised unit called Destroyer Division X-Ray under an inexperienced commander. The order went out at 0432hrs, but the six destroyers did not leave their screening position near the battleships until 0500hrs. In addition, both the left- and right-flank cruisers belatedly headed south at 15 knots accompanied by seven destroyers from Destroyer Squadron 56.

The American forces headed south were superior to Shima's force, but Oldendorf never pressed the advantage. He fought the entire battle with caution, primarily because he was uncertain as to the size of the force he was up against. Pre-battle intelligence estimates suggested there could be additional Japanese ships operating in the area as well as those already engaged. This caution ensured Shima would make good his escape. His force was steaming south at 18 knots—the best speed that *Nachi* could make. The escape of Nishimura's survivors was less certain. *Mogami* could only make 15 knots, so she fell behind Shima's force by 3,000 yards. *Asagumo*, without her bow, was some 6,000 yards north of Shima's cruisers. Only *Shigure* looked likely to make an escape.

Given her position and large radar signature, *Mogami* was the first ship encountered by Oldendorf's pursuing cruisers. At 0529hrs, *Portland* opened fire with her 8in. guns from 19,500 yards. Shima saw *Mogami* come under fire, but decided not to come to her assistance. *Portland*'s initial salvos were observed to straddle the target, which began to maneuver. Within minutes, *Louisville* and 6in. cruisers *Denver* and *Columbia* also joined in. This barrage resulted in at least ten more hits that created fires amidships and on the aft flight deck. *Minneapolis* gained contact on *Asagumo* at 0533hrs and hit the destroyer's stern, resulting in a fire and a reduction in speed to seven knots.

Both ships were given a respite when, at 0537hrs, Oldendorf ordered his cruisers to head north to avoid possible torpedoes from *Mogami*, followed by a ceasefire at 0539hrs. During the few minutes the cruisers had engaged *Mogami*, 197 8in. and 356 6in. shells were expended. The ceasefire provided another reprieve for *Mogami*. She fought off an attack by *PT-491* at 0600hrs with her two remaining 8in. turrets. Three more PTs attacked some 20 minutes later, but they were turned away by gunfire with the assistance of *Akebono* that had been ordered to escort the wounded cruiser to either Coron Bay or Cagayan. Oldendorf turned south again at 0617hrs and at 0643hrs ordered two light cruisers and three destroyers to finish off the damaged ships.

PT-321 picking up a Japanese survivor in Surigao Strait. Few Japanese elected to be taken prisoner. IJN personnel casualties aboard the six ships sunk from Nishimura's command totaled almost 4,100 men.

The last ship sunk by American surface forces was *Asagumo*. *PT-323* attacked the destroyer as the crew was abandoning ship, and one of her torpedoes struck *Asagumo* at 0702hrs. *Denver*, *Columbia*, and an eventual total of eight destroyers arrived and took *Asagumo* under fire just minutes later. The Japanese ship replied with her aft 5in. turret before sinking at 0721hrs. Most of her crew – 191 men – perished, but 39, including her commanding officer, got ashore and were later picked up by the Americans. As *Asagumo* slipped under the waves, all that was left of Nishimura's force were hundreds of survivors in the water. Rescue efforts by at least four American destroyers resulted in only a handful being picked up. When one of Oldendorf's destroyer skippers asked at 0735hrs what to do with the hundreds of men still in the water, Oldendorf simply replied, "Let them sink." Japanese survivors who reached shore were, in many cases, killed by local inhabitants.

Kinkaid and Oldendorf had more pressing concerns than the fate of Japanese survivors who refused rescue. A crisis to the north was becoming acute. Kurita's force had entered the Philippine Sea by way of San Bernardino Strait and encountered one of Kinkaid's three Escort Carrier Groups just before 0700hrs off Samar. Tremendously

Light cruiser *Denver* (left) firing on a target during the pursuit phase of the Battle of Surigao Strait. The burning ship on the right is destroyer *Asagumo*, which later sank with the loss of most of her crew. *Asagumo* was the only ship sunk by Oldendorf's surface forces during their uncertain pursuit.

outgunned, the commander of Taffy 3, Rear Admiral Clifton Sprague, began to plead for help minutes into the battle. As Kurita pressed his advantage, these pleas became more urgent. In response, Oldendorf recalled his advance guard at 0723hrs. Kinkaid ordered Oldendorf to bring his entire force north at 0847hrs to assist the escort carriers.

He formed a task force of the battleships *California*, *Tennessee*, and *Pennsylvania*, because they had the most armor-piercing shells remaining. They were escorted by three heavy cruisers and 20 destroyers with 165 torpedoes.

Of Kinkaid's three Escort Carrier Groups, the one located furthest to the south (and furthest from Kurita) was active throughout the morning against the Japanese forces fleeing from Surigao Strait. Taffy 1 launched its first strikes before 0600hrs. The first four Avengers from *Petrof Bay* found *Mogami* at 0741hrs. The cruiser fought her attackers fiercely, and none of the aircraft scored a hit with their bombs.

At around 0840hrs, *Nachi*, *Ashigara*, and destroyers *Shiranuhi* and *Kasumi* were attacked by 11 Avengers and ten Hellcats from carriers *Santee* and *Sangamon*. The Avengers all carried torpedoes and went after Shima's two cruisers that had been misidentified as Fuso-class battleships. Even with her reduced speed, *Nachi* successfully dodged all the torpedoes aimed at her. One of the Avengers from *Santee* was shot down. The only damage was to *Shiranuhi*, which was heavily strafed and suffered nine dead and 25 wounded.

The next strike consisting of ten Avengers, each with two 500lb bombs instead of torpedoes, escorted by five Wildcats, all from *Ommaney Bay*, went after *Mogami*. The Avenger pilots claimed five hits on the cruiser; in fact, only two bombs struck the ship. By the time the attack concluded at 0910hrs, *Mogami* was dead in the water after the failure of her last turbine. New fires raged beyond control and the danger of the forward 8in. magazine exploding (the others had been flooded) put the entire crew in danger. At 1030hrs, the acting captain gave the order to abandon ship. *Akebono* came alongside, in spite of the possibility of a magazine explosion, and took off the remaining crew. Then the destroyer fired a single Type 93 torpedo to scuttle the cruiser. *Mogami* sank at 1307hrs with the loss of 191 men, but another 700 were rescued by *Akebono*. *Mogami* had put up an epic fight. In spite of the fact that she had been hit by an estimated 100 shells, an explosion of her own torpedoes, three bomb hits, and the collision with *Nachi*, casualties had been relatively light.

Shigure was the only ship of Nishimura's force to survive. She was subjected to a final PT attack at 0648hrs, but was undamaged. Her skipper decided to forego Coron Bay and headed straight to Brunei Bay, where the destroyer arrived at 1700hrs on October 27.

Shima's two heavy cruisers and two destroyers made good their escape after several more PT attacks. The fate of *Abukuma* was not decided until later on October 26. After being torpedoed by a PT boat, *Abukuma* worked back up to 20 knots and later encountered Shima's formation. At 0830hrs *Abukuma* was ordered to head to Cagayan escorted by destroyer *Ushio*. The cruiser instead was diverted to the small port of Dapitan on northwest Mindanao at 2230hrs, where the crew made repairs throughout the night. The next morning, *Abukuma* and *Ushio* departed for Coron Bay. They did not get far. In the Sulu Sea, the two ships came under a series of attacks from a total of 43 B-24 heavy bombers. Usually high-altitude attacks on ships were totally ineffective, so the bombers came in at an altitude of about 6,500ft. In the first attack, *Abukuma* took a direct hit in the area of her bridge at 1006hrs and another aft. The second group of bombers scored a damaging near miss forward, and then a direct hit aft that knocked out one of the shafts and the steering equipment. The resulting fires spread to the engine rooms and the torpedo mounts located aft. When the fires reached the torpedoes, four exploded at 1037hrs. A third attack at 1044hrs brought only near misses. *Abukuma* was mortally damaged but remained afloat long enough for 284 of the crew to leave the ship. The veteran cruiser, part of the force that attacked Pearl Harbor, sank at 1242hrs with the loss of 220 men (added to the loss of 37 from the torpedo hit from the PT boat). As they came in at a lower altitude, *Abukuma* and *Ushio* were able to account for three bombers in this action.

Shiranuhi was sent back to assist light cruiser *Kinu* after it had been damaged following the conclusion of the counter-landing operation. The destroyer was sunk on October 27 south of Semirara Island with all hands. The last of Shima's force, destroyers *Akebono* and *Ushio*, arrived at Manila heavy with survivors.

Surigao Strait—a preordained victory?

Though it was not fully apparent to Kinkaid and Oldendorf at the time, they possessed an overwhelming numerical and firepower advantage over the Japanese. This advantage was magnified by geography that restricted Japanese maneuvering room and forced them to confront all the layers of Oldendorf's set-piece battle plan. Also not fully apparent to the Americans was the degree to which Japanese night-fighting skills had atrophied, so a gap had developed between the IJN and USN in night combat.

Surigao Strait was the last major night surface battle of the war. It was one of the worst performances (if not *the* worst) by the IJN in a night battle during the entire conflict. Despite having radar on all their ships, the IJN did not use it effectively. The usual Japanese prowess with night optics was also not in evidence; on several occasions American destroyers closed for torpedo attacks to which the Japanese did not even take evasive action. After the battle Japanese survivors believed that PT boats, not destroyers, were responsible for the many successful torpedo attacks, indicating they failed to grasp the threat posed by USN destroyers that used radar for torpedo attacks. Even harder to explain is the lack of aggressiveness displayed by both Nishimura's and Shima's forces. Destroyer *Shigure* left the battle without firing a single torpedo, as was the case with Shima's four destroyers. Japanese gunnery was lackluster, with only the secondary battery on *Yamashiro* able to score hits. Nishimura's two old battleships gave mixed performances, but overall they demonstrated why they were considered second-line units by the IJN. *Fuso* sank after taking only two torpedoes, while *Yamashiro* took a severe pounding before she finally sank. Her 14in. main battery failed to score a hit during the whole battle. The toughness displayed by *Mogami* speaks to the courage of Japanese sailors, but even this display of resilience made no contribution to victory.

Kinkaid and Oldendorf implemented a simple plan to maximize their firepower and geographic advantages. Radar was an essential element of the victory. It provided the Americans with overall situational awareness never possessed by the Japanese and critical targeting data for torpedoes and guns.

Unlike most night battles fought by the USN, the most effective American weapons at Surigao Strait were torpedoes. Destroyers and torpedo combat were highlighted in Oldendorf's plan, and the result was that Nishimura's force was shattered before it came into contact with Oldendorf's main strength.

Overshadowing the excellence of USN destroyers in the battle were the guns of Oldendorf's big ships. The battleships received considerable attention, since it was the last time these ships would engage an enemy surface target in naval history. *West Virginia*, *California*, and *Tennessee* were equipped with the Mk 8 fire control radar, which was the most advanced in the world. This was reflected by *West Virginia*'s gunnery, which scored a direct hit on *Yamashiro* on her first salvo. The three Mk 8-equipped ships fired the majority of the large-caliber rounds in the battle: *West Virginia* 93, *Tennessee* 69, and *California* 63. The three battleships carrying the older Mk 3 fire control radar were much less effective. *Maryland* fired only 48 rounds, probably with minimal accuracy since she was using the splashes of the other battleships as a target; *Mississippi* fired a single salvo of 12 rounds (the final salvo from a battleship against a battleship in naval history) and *Pennsylvania* did not fire at all.

THE BATTLE OFF CAPE ENGAÑO

The operations of Ozawa's Main Body
Ozawa's carrier force possessed little striking power. The four carriers entered the battle with only 116 aircraft, flown by largely untrained aviators. Ozawa planned to use whatever striking power he had to contribute to the weight of air attacks against TF 38 on October 24. On this day, Ozawa's morning search found nothing, but multiple contacts were generated by land-based aircraft on a USN carrier task force east of Luzon. Ozawa had enough aircraft for a single strike, and once launched, most aircraft were not able to land back on board their carriers. Upon receiving the initial contact reports, Ozawa declined

to launch his strike until he could confirm the enemy's location with one of his own search aircraft. This was received at 1115hrs with a report of a USN carrier task group only 180NM to the southwest of the Main Body. It is not flattering to TF 38 that a Japanese carrier force could steam to within 180NM of one of its task groups and remain undetected.

Ozawa was in no position to make TF 38 pay for its carelessness, but he was in a position to launch the final Japanese carrier strike of the war. It was so weak and disjointed that it was not even recognized by the Americans as the final attack of the IJN's once all-powerful carrier force. The Japanese launched 72 aircraft. *Zuikaku* contributed the most with ten Zero fighters, 11 Zero fighter-bombers, six torpedo bombers, and two reconnaissance aircraft. Of the 72, six went to Combat Air Patrol (CAP) and one aborted. This left 65 to head south toward TF 38. The strike group was ordered to proceed to Nichols Field on Luzon if bad weather made it impossible to return to the carriers. This was a concern, since the morning search missions had reported bad weather in the area of the USN carrier force.

The strike was directed at Sherman's TG 38.3. Earlier in the day, Japanese land-based aircraft damaged light carrier *Princeton*. When Ozawa's strike group arrived in the afternoon, the crews saw the burning carrier, but they were unable to add to the damage suffered by TG 38.3. After losing as many as 28 aircraft, the remainder headed for the Philippines with 33 landing on bases on Luzon and one proceeding to Formosa. Only three aircraft were able to return to their carrier.

In spite of the fact that the Main Body was operating within 200NM of TF 38, Ozawa's force was not spotted by the Americans. If the Main Body was detected, it could not perform its mission of drawing Halsey's force north. In order to ensure the Americans would detect his force, Ozawa formed a group designated Force A and sent it south at 1430hrs. This force, under Rear Admiral Matsuda Chiaki (commander of Carrier Division 4), was comprised of the battleships *Ise* and *Hyuga*, escorted by the four large Akizuki-class destroyers. Sending Force A south finally resulted in the initial detection of Ozawa's force. At about 1530hrs, it was spotted by American aircraft, and at 1635hrs Ozawa's carriers were also sighted. Ozawa was sure that he had been detected, since the uncoded transmission of the American contact report was intercepted. Given that the initial contact was made so late in the day, there was no possibility of an American strike on October 24. Ozawa sent a message at 1650hrs that he had been detected.

Halsey's decision
In the aftermath of the Battle of the Philippine Sea, the Americans did not know that the IJN had no prospects of replacing its lost aviators. Because the majority of the carriers themselves survived the battle, and the Americans knew other carriers were being added to the force, the IJN's carrier force was still a threat. The intelligence Halsey received on the IJN's carrier force indicated that it was fully capable. In every other major battle of the war, the IJN carrier fleet was the main threat. The Pacific War had become a carrier war and surface forces had been firmly supplanted as the primary striking force. The Americans had no way of knowing that the Japanese had turned this thinking on its head in their planning for Leyte Gulf.

Nimitz wanted to destroy the Combined Fleet and thus gain an increased measure of operational freedom for future operations. He was disappointed that this did not occur at Philippine Sea and thus had inserted the instruction to Halsey that the destruction of the Japanese fleet would be his primary objective if the opportunity was presented.

Halsey needed no instructions to aggressively seek out and destroy the Japanese fleet. The problem of how to destroy the Combined Fleet when it made an appearance would be in the execution. The Japanese had split their forces up, so Halsey had to decide which to attack. Further complicating matters was the late detection of the carrier force (reports of which Halsey received at about 1655hrs on October 24), after Kurita's and Nishimura's forces had already been detected and attacked.

As Kurita's force was clearly the bigger threat, it was bombarded by TF 38 on October 24. Reports from the aviators indicated the force had received considerable damage, so much so that it turned away to the west at about 1400hrs. The assessment from the aviators was that Kurita's force no longer posed a threat. However, Halsey had no way of knowing the degree to which his strikes had overly concentrated on *Musashi*, leaving most of Kurita's force battle ready. As Halsey knew, no surface could withstand that kind of pounding and remain a threat. After the air attacks were over, Kurita turned back to the east, which was tracked and reported back by night-capable aircraft from *Independence*. Unfortunately, Halsey and his staff dismissed these reports. By this point, after the late afternoon discovery of Ozawa's carrier force, Halsey had other things on his mind.

The last major Japanese force, Nishimura's, had been sighted and briefly attacked on the morning of October 24 as it headed to Surigao Strait. This force could be easily handled by Kinkaid's surface force.

Given all these factors, at 1950hrs Halsey ordered his entire force north to crush what he assessed as the primary threat—Ozawa's carrier force. He decided to do so with the entirety of his force—all three carrier task groups available to him and the battleships of TF 34. By so doing, he decided to ignore the threat posed by the Kurita force, which was headed toward San Bernardino Strait. He kept his whole force together, because that was how TF 38 fought and because, as he stated after the war, he did not want to divide his force in the face of the enemy. A decisive victory was most likely if the carriers of TF 38 worked with the battleships of TF 34. This was USN doctrine and Halsey fully supported it.

Destruction of the IJN's carrier force would constitute a decisive victory. Not only would it eliminate the main threat to the invasion, but it would cripple the IJN's ability to interfere with future operations.

Invariably, Halsey's logic that Ozawa's force was the primary threat, and that TF 38 had a golden opportunity to focus on it and destroy it met a host of real-world events that denied Halsey the battle of annihilation he had desired so much. At 1640hrs on October 24, Halsey alerted his task group commander to get ready to form TF 34. This was not an execution order, but it was picked up by Kinkaid who assumed it was. From this misconception, Kinkaid made several assumptions. He assumed that Halsey had formed TF 34. He assumed that this had been done with the purpose of defending San Bernardino Strait. He assumed that with San Bernardino Strait covered, he could focus on Surigao Strait, which he knew was the target of an advancing Japanese force of some strength.

Faced with at least two targets, Halsey should have divided his force to account for both. Certainly, TF 38 had the strength to do so. However, he resisted this notion for several reasons. First, it was against the principles of war to do so, as it gave the enemy the opportunity to defeat his force in detail. He considered leaving TF 34 and TG 38.2 to cover San Bernardino Strait, but decided against this because of the over-inflated threat from Japanese land-based aircraft. Most of all, he wanted to keep TF 38 concentrated to deliver a decisive blow against the IJN carrier force. In the end, Halsey chose to take his entire force to go after Ozawa. Not a single ship was left to defend or even watch San Bernardino Strait. The decision was relayed to Kinkaid, but was unclear and left the impression that TF 34 was left guarding San Bernardino Strait.

The orders to move TF 38 north were issued at 1950hrs. The disquieting information from one of *Independence*'s aircraft at 2005hrs that Kurita's force was again headed east prompted concern among several of Halsey's subordinates. Rear Admiral Bogan (commander of TG 38.2) and Vice Admiral Lee, commander of TF 34, were among those. Lee's signal that Kurita was the main threat was ignored by Halsey. Mitscher refused to even try to change Halsey's mind stating, "If he wants my advice, he'll ask for it."

While many of Halsey's subordinates had serious qualms with Halsey's plan to take his entire force north at the time, most criticism against Halsey has been made with the benefit of 20–20 hindsight. Had Halsey known that Ozawa's force was toothless and that the power of Japanese land-based aircraft had already been expended, it would have been obvious that Halsey should have divided his force and engaged both Ozawa's and Kurita's forces. Using the three carrier task forces and TF 34, a superior force could have been sent to engage both Japanese forces. This would have been a nuanced approach against Halsey's character, against existing USN doctrine, and against Halsey's ability to command distributed forces. Once Halsey had it in mind that the Japanese carrier force was the primary threat, Halsey's actions were virtually preordained.

The Battle off Cape Engaño

The result of Halsey's decision was that TF 38 headed north at 2022hrs. McCain's TG 38.1 was not included, since it was still steaming west from Ulithi, but the other three task groups still possessed an overwhelming advantage against Ozawa's force. Table 4 illustrates the disparity in power between the two forces.

Table 4: Forces participating in the Battle off Cape Engaño

Ship type	TG 38.2	TG 38.3	TG 38.4	Main Body
Fleet carriers	1	2	2	1
Light carriers	2	1	2	3
Operational aircraft	145	220	240	29
Battleships	2	2	2	2
Heavy cruisers	0	0	2	0
Light cruisers	3	3	0	3
Destroyers	16	14	11	8

With Halsey's 65 ships bearing down on Ozawa's 17, supported by an overwhelming advantage in aircraft, it was certain that Ozawa would pay a high price for successfully drawing Halsey away from Leyte. Ozawa expected that his force would be completely annihilated. This had been Halsey's dream since the start of the war—decisively engaging a Japanese carrier force. If he had been allowed to conduct the battle to its conclusion, Ozawa's force would have faced the real prospect of total annihilation. Here was another opportunity to put the doctrine of the Fast Carrier Task Force into action. The battle would open with a series of air strikes from ten fleet and light carriers. Following this blow, Task Force 34, with six battleships, two heavy cruisers, five light cruisers, and 18 destroyers, would finish off the cripples and chase down any survivors.

After the rendezvous of three of Halsey's four carrier task groups just before midnight on October 24, TF 38 headed north with every expectation of achieving a great victory. At 0100hrs on October 25, five radar-equipped aircraft flew off *Independence* to search out to a distance of 350NM. Contact was gained at 0205hrs on Force A and at 0235hrs on the Main Body. Because of a transmission error, the position of the Japanese forces was given incorrectly. The wrong position was plotted out some 120NM nearer to TF 38 than it actually was. In fact, TF 38 and Ozawa were actually about 210NM apart.

Throughout the night, the flight and hangar deck crews on TF 38's carriers prepared for the dawn launch of the first strike and CAP aircraft. The battle was fought under Mitscher who received tactical command of TF 38 just before midnight. At 0240hrs, TF 34 was formed with its impressive collection of six battleships and accompanying escorts. This was an intricate process that required the carriers to slow down so that the various ships from all three task groups could clear the formation and form a new one 10 miles north of flagship *Lexington*. Mitscher had to form TF 34 early on, since if Ozawa's force maintained its course, it would contact TF 38 as early as 0430hrs.

The *Independence* aircraft tracking Ozawa's force during the night lost contact when it was forced to break off because of engine problems. To regain contact, search aircraft were sent aloft at earliest dawn. A Hellcat from *Essex* gained contact on the now reunited Main Body at 0710hrs and sent an accurate contact report. The Japanese were only 150NM away, headed to the northeast at 20 knots. Mitscher was not content to wait for a contact report before he launched his first strike. The first deck loads of strike aircraft were launched between 0540hrs and 0600hrs concurrently with the search aircraft. As the search aircraft fanned out, the strike circled 50–70NM ahead of TF 38 waiting for word of the Main Body's location. Because the distance between the task forces was only about 145NM, when the 0710hrs contact report on the Main Body was issued, the American strike was

The Main Body maneuvers under air attack during the early stages of the Battle off Cape Engaño, seen from a *San Jacinto* Avenger. Note the bursts from Japanese Type 89 5in. guns. The patterns demonstrate the Japanese were using barrage fire, which was not effective against fast-moving carrier aircraft.

vectored toward it and arrived in an hour. The first strike went in at about 0830hrs under the direction of Commander David McCampbell, air group commander of Air Group 15 from *Essex*.

The Japanese were aware of the impending arrival of the initial strike, since radar aboard *Zuikaku* had detected the American aircraft at 0804hrs about 110NM to the southwest. Four Zeros were already on CAP; these were joined by the last nine fighters on *Zuikaku*. Such a meager CAP meant that survival of Ozawa's ships depended on their ability to throw up accurate antiaircraft fire and maneuver adeptly under dive-bombing and torpedo attack.

The bulk of the first strike came from TG 38.3's *Essex*, *Lexington*, and *Langley*. *Enterprise* from TG 38.4 contributed 36 aircraft—16 Hellcats, 13 Helldivers, and seven Avengers. In total, about 130 aircraft were involved. In excellent weather, the Americans had no problems spotting the Japanese formation at 0810hrs some 25NM ahead. McCampbell assigned targets after he observed the Main Body was operating in two groups; the northern group was centered on *Zuikaku* and *Zuiho* with a southern group built around *Chitose* and *Chiyoda*.

According to American pilots, Japanese antiaircraft fire was heavy and began with a display of multi-colored explosions at 15NM out as *Ise* and *Hyuga* fired *sanshiki-dan* incendiary shells from their 14in. main battery. The small Japanese CAP raced toward the approaching American formation, but the escorting Hellcats prevented them from reaching the Helldivers or Avengers. *Essex* Hellcats claimed nine Zeros, but one Hellcat was shot down and its pilot left in the water to witness the unfolding attack; he was rescued after the battle.

Beginning at about 0830hrs, and for the next hour, the Japanese ships came under unrelenting air attack. The Helldivers went in first, followed

The primary American target at Cape Engaño was fleet carrier *Zuikaku*. This is *Zuikaku* underway early in the action. Note the camouflage pattern on her flight deck and the heavy smoke issuing from her stacks.

by strafing Hellcats. Last to attack were the torpedo-laden Avengers. Ozawa's carriers were the main target.

Zuikaku came under attack from dive-bombers and torpedo bombers from *Intrepid*, and two light carriers. Five minutes into the attack, *Zuikaku* was hit by three bombs amidships, which created a fire on the lower and upper hangar decks. Just minutes later, a torpedo launched by an Avenger from either *Intrepid* or *San Jacinto* struck the ship on her port side. One of the engine rooms was flooded, and one of the shafts was damaged and had to be shut down. The ensuing flooding caused a severe list, but this was quickly corrected to a manageable 6°. The veteran carrier had an experienced and capable damage-control team. By 0850hrs, the fires were extinguished, and 23 knots were restored using the starboard shafts. However, steering was uneven, and the ship's transmitters were out of commission. Since she was no longer suitable as a flagship, plans were made to transfer Ozawa and his staff to cruiser *Oyodo*. Before this could happen, the second strike showed up.

Zuiho was caught out of formation launching aircraft when the first attack began. *Enterprise*'s strike group targeted the veteran light carrier known to her crew as a lucky ship, since she had survived three earlier carrier battles. Reports from *Enterprise* air crew stated that the carrier was left dead in the water and on fire. In exchange, one *Enterprise* Avenger was seriously damaged by antiaircraft fire and was rolled over the side of the carrier when it landed back onboard. Another *Enterprise* Hellcat was lost to Zero attack. *Intrepid* Helldivers also selected *Zuiho* for attack and claimed hits. In fact, *Zuiho* suffered three near misses followed by a direct bomb hit at 0835hrs. The explosion caused fires on the hangar deck, but these were out by 0855hrs. After the dive-bombers did their work, torpedo bombers from *Essex* and *Lexington* attacked *Zuiho*, but no hits were gained.

Light carrier *Chitose* was crippled early and was the first of Ozawa's carriers to sink. At 0835hrs, she was attacked by dive-bombers from *Essex* and *Lexington*. Helldivers from *Essex* reported dropping 12 bombs and claimed 8 hits, leaving the carrier burning and listing. In fact, *Chitose* suffered three near misses along her port side. This was enough to rupture the carrier's unarmored hull. The resulting flooding knocked out two boiler rooms and caused a severe 27° list. Damage-control efforts reduced the list and kept power, but steering was only accomplished by using the engines. At 0915hrs, progressive flooding knocked out the starboard engine room and speed fell below 14 knots. Ten minutes later, flooding caused all power to be lost and the list increased to a dangerous 30°. *Hyuga* was directed to tow the carrier, but her condition was beyond salvage. *Chitose* sank at 0937hrs with the loss of 904 officers and men; another 601 were saved.

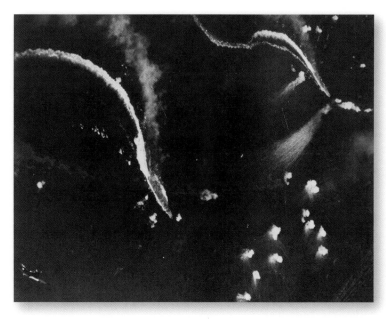

Carriers *Zuikaku* (left center) and *Zuiho* (right) under attack by American dive-bombers, seen from an *Enterprise* aircraft. Both ships are making good speed, indicating that this photograph was almost certainly taken during the first raid. Antiaircraft fire is heavy, but it appears to be ineffective. Note the Helldiver diving in the lower left part of the image.

THE BATTLE OFF CAPE ENGAÑO (PART 1)

Shown here are the opening phases of the battle on October 25, 1944, from 0800hrs to 1445hrs.

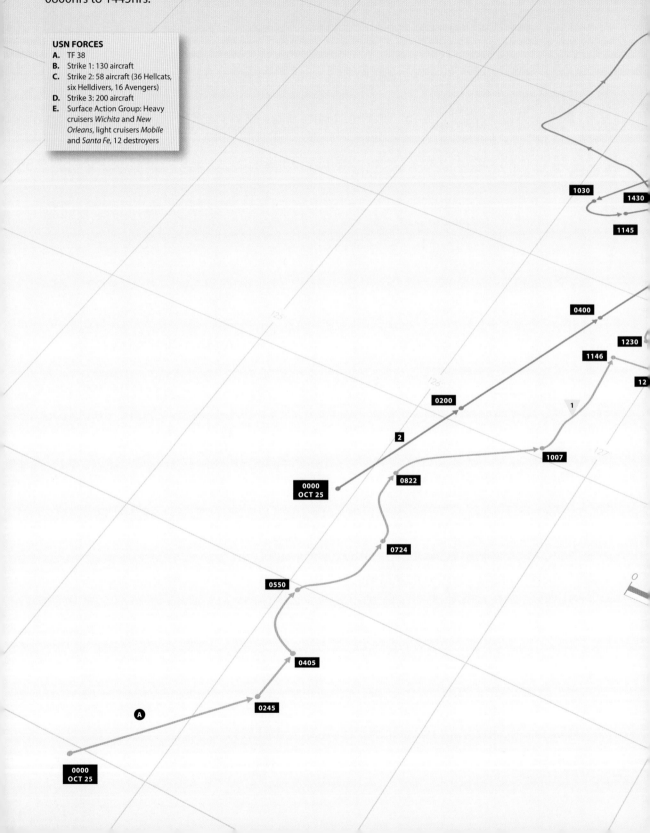

USN FORCES
A. TF 38
B. Strike 1: 130 aircraft
C. Strike 2: 58 aircraft (36 Hellcats, six Helldivers, 16 Avengers)
D. Strike 3: 200 aircraft
E. Surface Action Group: Heavy cruisers *Wichita* and *New Orleans*, light cruisers *Mobile* and *Santa Fe*, 12 destroyers

1030
1430
1145

0400
1230
1146
12

0200
1
2
1007

0822
0000
OCT 25

0724

0550

0405

0245

A

0000
OCT 25

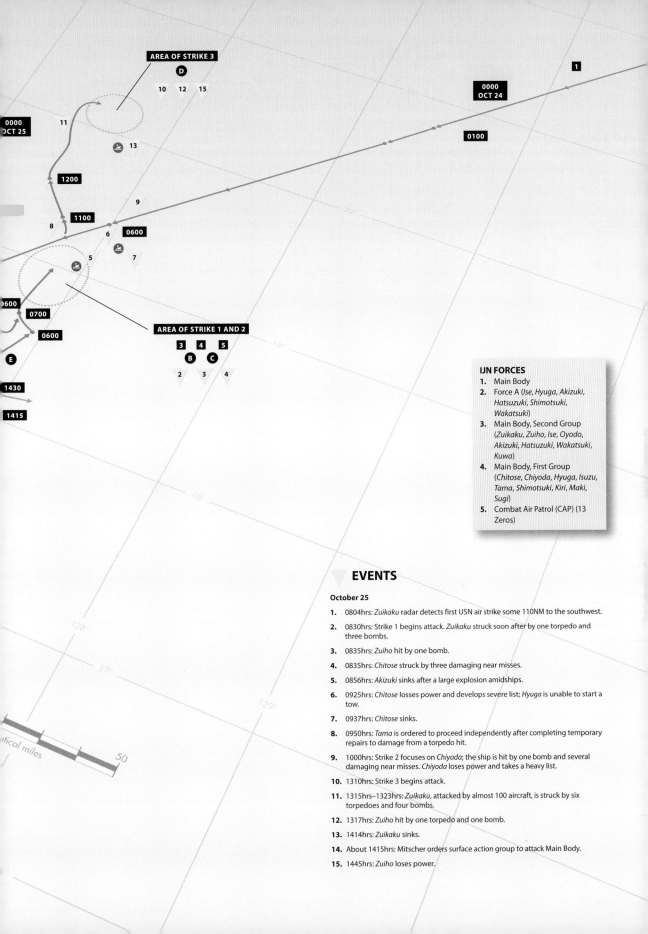

AREA OF STRIKE 3

D

10 12 15

1

0000
OCT 24

0100

0000
OCT 25

11

13

1200

9

1100

8

0600

6

5

7

0600

0700

0600

E

1430

1415

AREA OF STRIKE 1 AND 2

3 4 5

B C

2 3 4

IJN FORCES
1. Main Body
2. Force A (*Ise, Hyuga, Akizuki, Hatsuzuki, Shimotsuki, Wakatsuki*)
3. Main Body, Second Group (*Zuikaku, Zuiho, Ise, Oyodo, Akizuki, Hatsuzuki, Wakatsuki, Kuwa*)
4. Main Body, First Group (*Chitose, Chiyoda, Hyuga, Isuzu, Tama, Shimotsuki, Kiri, Maki, Sugi*)
5. Combat Air Patrol (CAP) (13 Zeros)

nautical miles

50

▼ **EVENTS**

October 25

1. 0804hrs: *Zuikaku* radar detects first USN air strike some 110NM to the southwest.

2. 0830hrs: Strike 1 begins attack. *Zuikaku* struck soon after by one torpedo and three bombs.

3. 0835hrs: *Zuiho* hit by one bomb.

4. 0835hrs: *Chitose* struck by three damaging near misses.

5. 0856hrs: *Akizuki* sinks after a large explosion amidships.

6. 0925hrs: *Chitose* losses power and develops severe list; *Hyuga* is unable to start a tow.

7. 0937hrs: *Chitose* sinks.

8. 0950hrs: *Tama* is ordered to proceed independently after completing temporary repairs to damage from a torpedo hit.

9. 1000hrs: Strike 2 focuses on *Chiyoda*; the ship is hit by one bomb and several damaging near misses. *Chiyoda* loses power and takes a heavy list.

10. 1310hrs: Strike 3 begins attack.

11. 1315hrs–1323hrs: *Zuikaku*, attacked by almost 100 aircraft, is struck by six torpedoes and four bombs.

12. 1317hrs: *Zuiho* hit by one torpedo and one bomb.

13. 1414hrs: *Zuikaku* sinks.

14. About 1415hrs: Mitscher orders surface action group to attack Main Body.

15. 1445hrs: *Zuiho* loses power.

Chitose's damaged condition prompted McCampbell to redirect the Avengers he had originally ordered to attack the carrier. Of the 16 Avengers reporting an attack on carriers or battleships, ten claimed hits. In fact, only the single torpedo hit on *Zuikaku* was confirmed by Japanese sources.

In addition to the three carriers, some of the escorts came under attack. Light cruiser *Tama* was attacked by torpedo bombers from *Belleau Wood* and *San Jacinto*. One torpedo hit the ship in her boiler room. After emergency repairs, the cruiser was ordered to proceed independently to Okinawa at her best speed of 14 knots. *Oyodo* was also subjected to attack and was slightly damaged. At 0848hrs, she was struck by a bomb and two rockets and recorded near misses from bombs. The cruiser's speed was unimpaired.

Large destroyer *Akizuki* also came under attack from aircraft in the first strike. At 0842hrs the ship was struck amidships and set afire. The ship lost power and fell out of formation. Within minutes, a large explosion was noted amidships and at 0856hrs *Akizuki* broke in two and quickly sank. The cause was either a torpedo or a bomb hit that detonated torpedoes in the amidships torpedo mount. The commanding officer and 150 officers and men were pulled out of the water before more air attacks forced destroyer *Maki* to abandon rescue operations.

A second strike took off at around 0835hrs and arrived in the target area at about 0945hrs. This was comprised of 36 aircraft (14 Hellcats, six Helldivers, and 16 Avengers) from *Lexington*, *Franklin*, *Langley*, *San Jacinto*, and *Belleau Wood* from TGs 38.3 and 38.4. McCampbell remained active as target coordinator. When the strike arrived, it found the Main Body in disarray. McCampbell selected the undamaged *Chiyoda* for attack. Aircraft from *Lexington* and *Franklin* delivered the attack, and at 1000hrs the carrier was hit by a bomb on the port quarter of the flight deck while damaging near misses were recorded on the starboard side. The magazines were flooded as a precaution after fires broke out. This, and the hull damage

At about 1100hrs, Vice Admiral Ozawa departed the damaged *Zuikaku*. This view shows light cruiser *Oyodo* approaching the carrier's port quarter to receive the admiral and his staff.

from the near misses, created a 13° starboard list. The flooding reached the starboard engine room, which brought *Chiyoda* to a stop. *Hyuga* and destroyers *Shimotsuki* and *Maki* were ordered to assist. *Hyuga* prepared to tow the 11,200-ton carrier, but the attempt was suspended when the third strike was spotted. At 1414hrs *Isuzu* returned to start a tow, but she was hit by a bomb forward of the bridge. More attacks and a lack of fuel forced *Isuzu* to give up. Steering problems made it impossible for the light cruiser to close and pick up *Chiyoda's* crew. Later, *Isuzu* was ordered to return to pick up the crew and sink the carrier with torpedoes. At 1548hrs, as *Isuzu* approached *Chiyoda's* position, the carrier was observed to be under

This view is probably of *Chiyoda* under attack from *Lexington* or *Franklin* aircraft during the second raid. The second raid focused on *Chiyoda*, and bomb damage brought her to a stop. Both *Chiyoda* and sistership *Chitose* suffered damage from bomb near misses, but this was enough to penetrate their unprotected hulls and cause fatal or severe damage.

surface attack. *Isuzu* reversed course to the north, leaving *Chiyoda* to her fate.

Launched between 1145hrs and 1200hrs, the third strike was the largest and most effective of the day. It was active over the target area from about 1310hrs to 1400hrs with some 200 aircraft, 75 percent of which had taken part in the initial strike in the morning. The strike coordinator was Commander T. Hugh Winters from *Lexington*. By this point, the Main Body's formation was in a shambles. Two carriers were located to the north with a battleship and what was reported as two cruisers. Another carrier was located some 20NM to the south on fire and listing. A second battleship, a cruiser, and a destroyer were nearby the crippled carrier.

Winters ordered TG 38.3's 98 aircraft from *Essex*, *Lexington*, and *Langley*, to go after the two operational carriers. Aircraft from *Lexington* focused on *Zuikaku*. By 1100hrs, Ozawa had departed his flagship and transferred to *Oyodo*. The nine surviving Zeros on CAP were forced to ditch around 1030hrs, so for the rest of the day the Americans faced no air

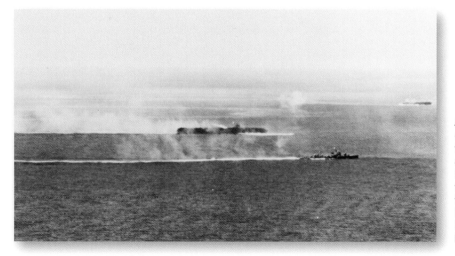

Zuikaku and an Akizuki-class destroyer maneuver during the third attack from TF 38 aircraft. The time of the photo is about 1330hrs, which means the carrier has already received fatal damage that resulted in her sinking less than an hour later. *Zuiho* can be seen in the background on the right.

Jim Laurier

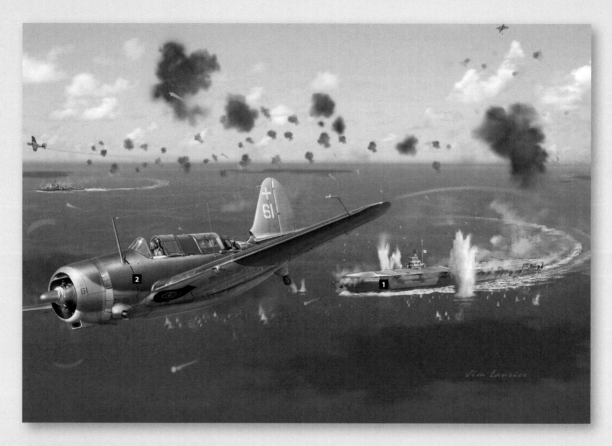

ZUIKAKU UNDER AIR ATTACK (PP.74–75)

The most lucrative target awaiting Halsey's aviators on the morning of October 25 was fleet carrier *Zuikaku*, veteran of four of the war's five carrier battles. In the first strike, *Zuikaku* was attacked by dive-bombers and Avengers from *Intrepid*, and two light carriers. The small Japanese combat air patrol was ineffective in defending the carrier, which was now left to defend against the attack with antiaircraft fire and adept evasive maneuvering.

This scene shows *Zuikaku* (1) in a high-speed turn to port. The smoke is from the ship's battery of 96 25mm antiaircraft guns. Note the camouflage on the flight deck; all four of Ozawa's carriers at Cape Engaño wore similar patterns. Only minutes

into the attack *Zuikaku*'s flight deck was hit by three bombs. The bombs started a fire on the two hangar decks, which took some 15 minutes to extinguish. Most of the 1,000lb bombs from the Helldivers (2) missed, as shown in this scene.

After the Helldivers had done their work, the Avengers hit the big carrier with a torpedo on her port side between elevators Number 2 and 3. The ensuing flooding caused a temporary list of almost 30°, but this was quickly reduced to a manageable 6°. *Zuikaku* survived the first strike; however, the larger third strike concentrated on her and delivered a devastating barrage of six torpedo and four bomb hits. By 1414hrs, *Zuikaku* was gone.

opposition. *Zuikaku* worked up to 24 knots shortly after the third strike was spotted at 1308hrs. The attack by Helldivers and Avengers was well coordinated, with the Avengers coming in from both bows in an anvil attack. In less than ten minutes, *Zuikaku* was subjected to six torpedo hits—two on the starboard side and four on the port side. The first was a hit at 1315hrs that failed to detonate. The last of the six hit at 1323hrs. Within minutes of the last torpedo hit, the mighty carrier was listing to port by 14° and was dead in the water after all power was lost. In addition to the torpedoes, four bombs hit the ship, which resulted in renewed fires on the hangar decks. At 1327, with the list increasing to 21°, the crew was ordered up to the flight deck. The captain gave a final address and then the ensign was lowered. Finally, after this touch of the dramatic, the crew was ordered to abandon ship at 1358hrs. The ship rolled over at 1414hrs and took the captain, 48 other officers, and 794 enlisted men with her.

Essex's strike focused on *Zuiho*. When aircraft from TG 38.4 arrived, including *Enterprise*'s second strike of six Hellcats, ten Helldivers, and five Avengers, most were also directed at *Zuiho* at 1310hrs followed by more at 1330hrs. At 1317hrs, the carrier was hit by one torpedo on her starboard quarter. According to Japanese accounts, one small bomb hit the aft elevator, followed by seven very close near misses, and then 60 more near misses. Bomb fragments caused flooding in the starboard engine room and created a 13° list. By 1445hrs, the port engine room had flooded, which left the ship with no power. Though crippled, the carrier was attacked

This image was also taken during the third attack on the Main Body. *Zuikaku* (left center) is dead in the water and smoking; she will soon sink. *Zuiho* (left) is visible on fire; she has also taken fatal damage.

The end of *Zuikaku* as seen from USN carrier aircraft during the third attack on Ozawa's Main Body. The carrier has taken as many as six torpedo hits and has developed a heavy list to port. Note the Avenger torpedo plane in the foreground.

Crewmembers aboard *Zuikaku* salute as the Japanese naval ensign is lowered just minutes before the carrier sank at 1414hrs. In spite of the obvious heavy list, the captain insisted on this touch of the dramatic. This gesture was idiotic, since over 800 men were unable to get clear of the ship when she sank.

again in the fourth strike with another ten near misses being recorded. By 1500hrs, the list had increased to 23°, so the captain ordered the crew off the ship. The veteran carrier sank at 1526hrs. Seven officers and 208 enlisted men were lost, but an escorting destroyer saved a total of 759 men.

A few aircraft, including some from *Franklin*, attacked the ships around the crippled *Chiyoda*. The escorts were observed leaving the stationary carrier at about 1410hrs. No aircraft were reported lost in the third strike, but at least one *Essex* Helldiver returned so badly damaged it was dumped over the side.

One of the most iconic pictures of the entire war was provided by an Avenger from *Enterprise*. During the third attack on the Main Body, the aircraft was able to take a series of high-quality shots of *Zuiho* in action. This shows the carrier's flight deck with its dramatic camouflage as she desperately maneuvers.

Mitscher's fourth strike of the day was launched at about 1315hrs and reached the target area at about 1445hrs. It was comprised of 40 aircraft from *Essex*, *Lexington*, and *Langley*. Despite the fact that she was dead in the water, 27 aircraft went after *Zuiho*, but they could only add ten near misses to the carrier's catalog of damages. The dive-bomber squadron from *Essex* attacked *Ise* and claimed eight hits. The old battleship put up a very heavy barrage of antiaircraft fire, according to American pilots. Only four near misses were confirmed by the Japanese.

The next effort consisted of a large strike launched at 1610hrs with aircraft from the five fleet carriers. The 85 aircraft in the fifth strike did their work in the target area between 1710hrs and 1740hrs. For most of the pilots, this was their third strike of the day, and the results demonstrated their fatigue. As the largest ships present, the two hybrid battleship-carriers were attacked by almost all the aircraft present, with only two other escorts coming under ineffective attack. *Ise*, located in the area of the Main Body, received the most attention. Japanese accounts have her undergoing attack by 85 dive-bombers and 11 torpedo bombers. All 11 torpedoes were dodged, and only a single bomb hit outboard of the port catapult. The Japanese recorded an incredible 34 near misses, which caused the outer hull plates to rupture, resulting in minor flooding. Five crewmen were killed and 71

This is another in the series of remarkable photographs taken by the *Enterprise* Avenger. *Zuiho* has already been damaged as evinced by the buckled flight deck amidships and the heavy smoke issuing from the carrier's starboard quarter. Some of the smoke is from the downward-angled stack located in this area, but some was due to a single torpedo hit in the same area and a bomb that hit near the aft aircraft elevator.

This view of *Zuiho* shows the carrier under attack from *Essex* aircraft during the third raid. Note the large number of bomb explosions around the carrier. Near misses created damage to the ship's unprotected hull and resulted in flooding.

THE BATTLE OFF CAPE ENGAÑO (PART 2)

Shown here are the closing phases of the battle, from 1445hrs to 2130hrs on
October 25, 1944.

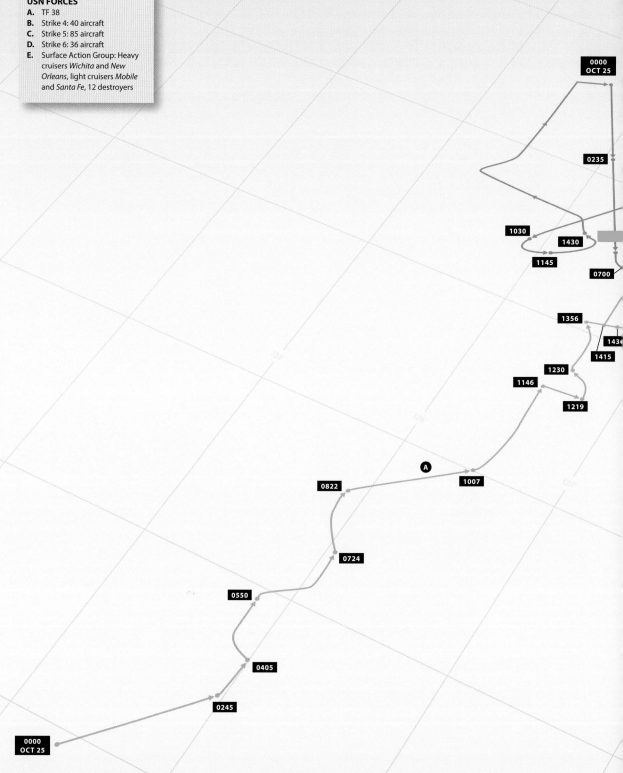

USN FORCES
A. TF 38
B. Strike 4: 40 aircraft
C. Strike 5: 85 aircraft
D. Strike 6: 36 aircraft
E. Surface Action Group: Heavy
    cruisers *Wichita* and *New
    Orleans*, light cruisers *Mobile*
    and *Santa Fe*, 12 destroyers

0000 OCT 25

0235

1030

1430

1145

0700

1356

1430

1415

1230

1146

1219

A

0822

1007

0724

0550

0405

0245

0000 OCT 25

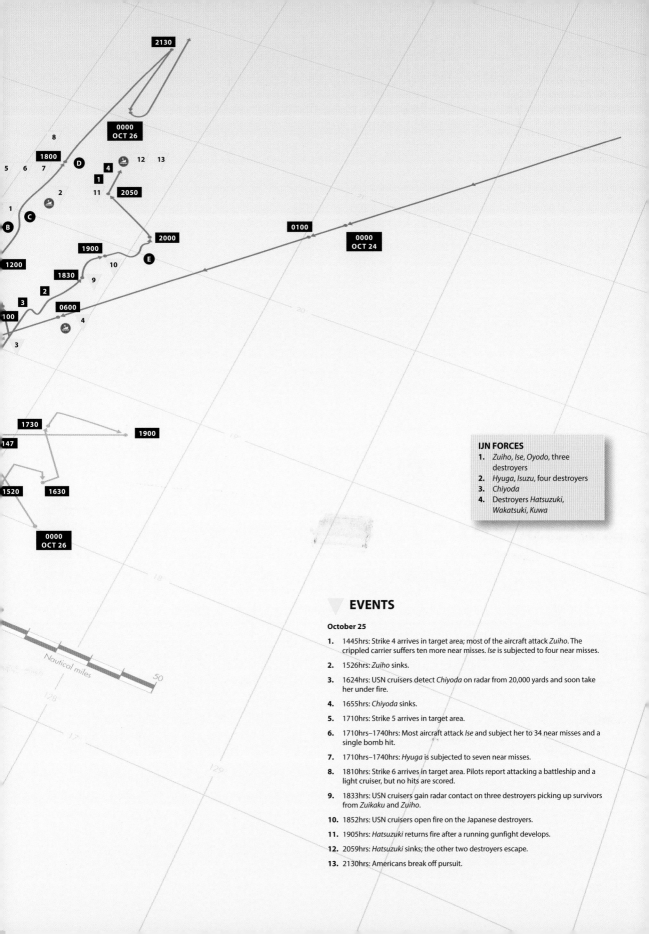

2130

0000
OCT 26

8

1800

5   6   7   D

2

1   C

B

12   13

4

1

11   2050

2000

1900

1830

10   E

9

2

1200

3

100

0600

4

3

0100

0000
OCT 24

1730

147   1900

1520   1630

0000
OCT 26

Nautical miles   50   0

IJN FORCES

1.   *Zuiho, Ise, Oyodo*, three
     destroyers
2.   *Hyuga, Isuzu*, four destroyers
3.   *Chiyoda*
4.   Destroyers *Hatsuzuki,
     Wakatsuki, Kuwa*

▼ **EVENTS**

October 25

1.   1445hrs: Strike 4 arrives in target area; most of the aircraft attack *Zuiho*. The
     crippled carrier suffers ten more near misses. *Ise* is subjected to four near misses.

2.   1526hrs: *Zuiho* sinks.

3.   1624hrs: USN cruisers detect *Chiyoda* on radar from 20,000 yards and soon take
     her under fire.

4.   1655hrs: *Chiyoda* sinks.

5.   1710hrs: Strike 5 arrives in target area.

6.   1710hrs–1740hrs: Most aircraft attack *Ise* and subject her to 34 near misses and a
     single bomb hit.

7.   1710hrs–1740hrs: *Hyuga* is subjected to seven near misses.

8.   1810hrs: Strike 6 arrives in target area. Pilots report attacking a battleship and a
     light cruiser, but no hits are scored.

9.   1833hrs: USN cruisers gain radar contact on three destroyers picking up survivors
     from *Zuikaku* and *Zuiho*.

10. 1852hrs: USN cruisers open fire on the Japanese destroyers.

11. 1905hrs: *Hatsuzuki* returns fire after a running gunfight develops.

12. 2059hrs: *Hatsuzuki* sinks; the other two destroyers escape.

13. 2130hrs: Americans break off pursuit.

After all four of Ozawa's carriers were sunk or crippled by air attack, the primary American targets shifted to the two Ise-class hybrid carrier-battleships. This image shows one of those ships under attack. Despite their relatively slow speed and indifferent maneuverability, only one bomb hit the pair throughout October 25.

Both *Ise* and *Hyuga* fought well against incessant air attack. In this view, one of the two ships can be seen firing back at her attackers. The heavy smoke is from the ship's huge number of 25mm guns—excessive smoke was one of the weapon's many faults. Note that the forward 14in. turret has just fired. The Japanese fired large-caliber shells in front of approaching Avengers to knock them down or disrupt their aim.

wounded. Heavy antiaircraft fire and adept maneuvering by *Ise*'s skipper, combined with pilot fatigue, prevented major damage. Sister ship *Hyuga*, steaming south of the Main Body, was also attacked. She suffered seven near misses, but not a single hit.

As the last strike aircraft departed, Ozawa's force was in peril of annihilation. *Ise*, *Oyodo*, and three destroyers were recovering *Zuiho* survivors from the water. Another group of *Hyuga*, light cruiser *Isuzu*, and a couple of destroyers were to the south of the Main Body. The wounded *Tama* was proceeding independently, trailing oil. Far to the south by some 60NM was the derelict *Chiyoda*.

The final strike was comprised of 36 aircraft from TG 38.4, including 16 Hellcats from *Enterprise*, each carrying a 1,000lb bomb. Taking off at 1710hrs, they arrived in the target area about one hour later. *Enterprise* pilots reported attacking a ship identified as a light cruiser and claimed five hits and three near misses. The other eight Hellcats attacked a battleship. According to Japanese sources, none of the aircraft from the sixth strike gained a hit.

Throughout the day, TF 38 mounted a total of 527 sorties against Ozawa's force, making this the most intensive effort by the fast carriers against naval

targets up to that time. To put this in context, the operations on October 25 against the Main Body was twice as large as the strikes against Kurita's force the day before. Given that the strikes faced virtually no air opposition and heavy but generally ineffective antiaircraft fire, the total damage on the Japanese must be seen as disappointing. Four carriers were sunk or crippled, a destroyer was sunk, major damage was inflicted on a light cruiser, and several other ships suffered light damage. All this was accomplished at the cost of ten aircraft lost to antiaircraft fire and a handful lost to Zeros. Ozawa stated after the war that the last three strikes were not damaging. His chief of staff went further and commented that he was not impressed with the quality of American pilots. Three reasons contributed to this relatively modest return on what was a massive effort: heavy antiaircraft fire, good ship handling, and fatigue on the part of TF 38 aircrew. American after action reports confirmed that pilot fatigue was a major factor in operations. It must be kept in mind that many TF 38 pilots had flown five missions in two days against the heaviest antiaircraft barrages in naval history.

An Ise-class battleship maneuvers with an Akizuki-class destroyer, as seen from a *San Jacinto* Avenger. Note the damaged wingtip of the aircraft. Despite the heavy volume of Japanese antiaircraft fire, only ten of 527 aircraft that attacked the Main Body were shot down by antiaircraft fire on October 25.

Mop-up by TF 38 surface forces

Halsey intended to have TF 34 finish off any remaining units of the Main Body. This dream came to an end at 1115hrs when the bulk of TF 34 turned south to render assistance to the Seventh Fleet. When it was clear that Ozawa's two battleships were headed north, Mitscher ordered a cruiser–destroyer force to finish off any Japanese cripples. This force, under the

CHIYODA **UNDER SURFACE ATTACK (PP.84–85)**

During World War II, it was exceedingly rare for aircraft carriers to come under attack from surface ships. The first to be sunk by surface attack was Royal Navy carrier *Glorious* off Norway in June 1940. The next, and last two, both occurred on October 25 during the Battle of Leyte Gulf. During the morning, Taffy 3 was attacked by a large force of IJN combatants. *Gambier Bay* was sunk by gunfire and several other escort carriers damaged. In the afternoon, USN surface units from TF 38 caught up with the crippled ships from Vice Admiral Ozawa's Main Body. Light carrier *Chiyoda* was crippled earlier in the day during the second American strike on the Main Body and was left dead after the ship lost power. Vice Admiral Mitscher ordered a force of four cruisers and 12 destroyers under Rear Admiral DuBose to dispatch any

cripples. DuBose's force first encountered *Chiyoda* with light cruiser *Isuzu* standing nearby preparing to rescue survivors. The heavily out-gunned *Isuzu* quickly fled. At 1624hrs, heavy cruisers *Wichita* and *New Orleans* opened fire with their 8in. guns at a range of 20,000 yards. Light cruisers *Mobile* and *Santa Fe* joined in the barrage and within 15 minutes, *Chiyoda* was a mass of flames.

This scene shows *Mobile* (**1**) and *New Orleans* (**2**) steaming in column and taking the carrier under fire. *Chiyoda* (**3**) burns in the background. The shell splashes in the foreground are from *Chiyoda*'s Type 89 5in. dual-purpose guns, which have opened up with an ineffective response. At 1655hrs, *Chiyoda* rolled over and sank, taking her entire crew of 970 men with her. She was the last of the four Japanese carriers lost that day.

command of Rear Admiral L.T. DuBose, possessed considerable strength with heavy cruisers *Wichita* and *New Orleans*, light cruisers *Santa Fe* and *Mobile*, and 12 destroyers.

DuBose's force first encountered *Chiyoda* dead in the water with light cruiser *Isuzu* nearby preparing to rescue survivors. *Isuzu* quickly fled, leaving the heavy cruisers to open fire at *Chiyoda* at 1624hrs from some 20,000 yards. The carrier responded with her 5in. dual-purpose guns, but against a stationary target the American cruiser scored quickly and often and after 15 minutes the carrier was a mass of flames. A towering column of black smoke marked *Chiyoda*'s final moments. At 1655hrs, the carrier rolled over—there were no survivors from her crew of 970 men.

As the American cruisers headed north in a column with the flanking destroyers arranged in four groups of three, at 1833hrs *Wichita* gained a distant radar contact at 35,200 yards. This was the two large destroyers *Hatsuzuki* and *Wakatsuki* and the smaller *Kuwa* that were in the process of picking up survivors from *Zuikaku* and *Zuiho*. At 1852hrs the Japanese were again surprised when the light cruisers opened up on *Hatsuzuki*, which was the nearest target. The longer-ranged 8in. guns on the heavy cruisers were assigned to hit the *Wakatsuki* and *Kuwa* at 28,200 yards, but this was too far for effective fire. *Hatsuzuki* returned fire at 1905hrs with her 3.9in. guns as the outgunned Japanese were fleeing north.

The Americans increased speed to 30 knots and maintained a stream of fire on the fleeing *Hatsuzuki*. The destroyer feinted several torpedo attacks and laid smoke to slow down her pursuers. This was sufficient to save *Wakatsuki* and *Kuwa*, but DuBose's ships continued to gain on *Hatsuzuki*. A torpedo attack from three American destroyers from 6,800 yards was unsuccessful, but the torrent of fire from 6in. and 8in. guns from about the same range eventually tore the destroyer apart. *Hatsuzuki* fought back bravely but ineffectively. She placed shells near two of the American cruisers,

The first ship encountered by the pursuing Americans under Rear Admiral DuBose was carrier *Chiyoda*, which had been crippled in the second air attack of the day. Several attempts during the day by Japanese ships to tow the carrier and save its crew were unsuccessful. American cruisers quickly pummeled the stationary carrier, shown burning in this view, and *Chiyoda* sank with no survivors.

After sinking *Chiyoda*, DuBose encountered a group of Japanese destroyers. The American were only able to chase down one, *Hatsuzuki*, and after a running battle sank the Japanese ship by gunfire. This image shows light cruiser *Mobile* firing on *Hatsuzuki*.

but she failed to hit anything. The destroyer took her final plunge at 2059hrs. From her crew of about 330, there were eight survivors, joined by 17 more survivors from *Zuikaku*.

DuBose broke off his pursuit at 2130hrs. This timing was fortuitous, since *Hatsuzuki*'s calls for help prompted Ozawa to head south with *Ise*, *Hyuga*, *Oyodo*, and destroyer *Shimotsuki* at 2041hrs. Finding nothing, Ozawa turned back at 2330hrs, bringing the battle to a close.

American submarine attacks

Though the Battle off Cape Engaño was over, the Japanese Main Body still had to run the final gauntlet. By this period in the war, the Pacific Fleet's submarine force, under Vice Admiral Charles Lockwood, had enough submarines to maintain the pressure on Japanese merchant traffic and provide direct support to major fleet operations. Picking up downed aviators was also a mission to which submarines had become proficient. Lockwood deployed 22 submarines around the Philippines, and since several were stationed in or near the important chokepoint of Luzon Strait, they were in a position to strike Ozawa's fleeing force.

Mitscher gave Lockwood notice of the battle area and the composition of Ozawa's force. Lockwood had already moved two wolf packs to form a scouting line on Ozawa's predicted path of retreat. *Pintado*, *Jallao*, and *Atule* were stationed along the eastern part of the line with *Haddock*, *Tuna*, and *Halibut* manning the western part. The first of a series of encounters occurred at 1742hrs when *Halibut* spotted *Ise* at 31,000 yards coming toward her. As the Japanese approached, *Halibut* went to periscope depth and also sighted

Oyodo and a destroyer. A full salvo of six torpedoes was directed at *Ise* at 1844hrs. The crew thought it heard five explosions, followed by the noises of a ship breaking up, but *Ise* was undamaged. *Haddock* also chased contacts reported as *Ise* and *Hyuga*, but could not get into firing position. *Halibut* got another shot at 2300hrs when she reported *Hyuga* and four destroyers, but she failed to get into firing position after a seven-hour chase.

The only success against Ozawa's force was scored by the brand-new boat *Jallao*. At 2004hrs, she gained radar contact on what turned out to be *Tama*. The cruiser was proceeding independently to Okinawa at 14 knots after taking a torpedo in the first air attack. *Jallao*'s skipper fired three torpedoes from her bow tubes, but they all missed. He quickly lined up another shot with the four stern tubes. Three of the four hit, and two exploded. The damage was catastrophic, causing *Tama* to break in two and quickly sink. There were no survivors from the crew of some 450 men.

TF 38 goes south

The climax of Halsey's battle of annihilation against the Main Body should have been an engagement by TF 34 with six of the world's most powerful battleships. But this was never to be. The plight of the escort carriers off Samar brought a flurry of urgent pleas to Halsey for assistance. These began at 0707hrs with a plain text message from Kinkaid. In response, Halsey ordered TG 38.1 to steam west from Ulithi to support Kinkaid, but otherwise remained focused on crushing Ozawa with the rest of TF 38. This changed when Nimitz weighed in at 1000hrs with an inquiry on the location of TF 34. This finally prompted him to order TF 34, supported by TG 38.2, south at 1015hrs. At this point, TF 34 was some 42NM away from Ozawa's remnants. This order was executed at 1115hrs when the battleships turned south. This change of orders for TF 34 came too late. Even at their best speed, the battle line could not arrive off San Bernardino Strait until about 0100hrs on October 26. At 1345hrs, TF 34 slowed from 20 to 12 knots to fuel destroyers. This took until 1622hrs. In a final attempt to cut off Kurita's force before it got through the strait, Halsey formed a fast element of TF 34 comprised of battleships *Iowa* and *New Jersey*, three light cruisers, and eight destroyers and ordered it to proceed at 28 knots to the strait. This fast element was designated TG 34.5 and was placed under the command of Rear Admiral Oscar Badger. The newly formed TG 34.5 was supported by TG 38.1 with its three carriers.

Badger's force arrived off San Bernardino Strait at 0100hrs on October 26. Since Kurita had slipped through some three hours earlier, Badger followed his orders to sweep south along the coast of Samar. The only Japanese ship in the area was destroyer *Nowaki*. She had fallen behind Kurita's main body after rescuing the survivors of heavy cruiser *Chikuma*.

Destroyer *Lewis Hancock* was sent to scout ahead of TG 34.5 and gained radar contact at 0028hrs on *Nowaki*. Halsey prudently kept his battleships out of a night engagement and instead ordered his three light cruisers and two destroyers to deal with the contact. With the benefit of radar, the Americans tracked the oblivious *Nowaki* before the cruisers opened fire with their 6in. guns at 0054hrs from a range of 18,300 yards. A short barrage failed to bring the target to a stop, so at 0101hrs all three cruisers, joined by the two destroyers, reopened fire. This had the desired effect; *Nowaki* was hit and came to a stop. Two American destroyers were ordered to finish *Nowaki*. After a failed attempt to do so with torpedoes, they closed in to use their 5in. guns at point-blank range. The Japanese destroyer could only manage a few ineffective salvos in return. Finally, at 0132hrs, a massive explosion was observed, and the destroyer sank minutes later. The fate of *Nowaki* provides a microcosm of the entire battle. For the IJN, it was just another in a long list of tragedies. When the destroyer sank, it did so with its entire crew of 240 men and all survivors from heavy cruiser *Chikuma*—the vast majority of 874 crewmen. For the Americans, the sinking of *Nowaki* was the only time surface ships from the Third Fleet engaged ships of the First Diversion Attack Force.

THE JAPANESE COUNTER-LANDING OPERATION

A footnote to the four major engagements comprising the Battle of Leyte Gulf was the fate of the Southwest Area Fleet Guard Force under Vice Admiral Naomasa Sakonju. This force was comprised of *Sentai* 16, consisting of heavy cruiser *Aoba*, light cruiser *Kinu*, and destroyer *Uranami*. These were assigned to escort three T.1-class fast transports, the Japanese version of destroyer transports, and two LSTs.

At 1700hrs on October 21, *Sentai* 16 was detached from Kurita's force to assist in the movement of the 41st Infantry Regiment from Cagayan, Mindanao to Ormoc on the western side of Leyte. On October 23, the small force was tracked by submarine *Bream* in the approaches to Manila Bay. At 0324hrs, the submarine got into position to fire six torpedoes at *Aoba*. One hit the cruiser in the engine room, bringing her to a stop and creating a list. *Kinu* towed her into Cavite Navy Yard. The cruiser eventually returned to Japan, but she was never fully operational again.

On October 24, *Kinu* and *Uranami* departed Cavite for Cagayan with the five transports. They were soon attacked by aircraft from *Lexington* and *Essex* of TG 38.3. No direct hits were gained, but the ships were heavily strafed, killing 47 on *Kinu* and 25 on *Uranami*. The force arrived at Cagayan the same evening where *T 6*, *T 9*, and *T 10* embarked 350 men each and *T 101* and *T 102* 400 each. The transports departed Cagayan on the morning of October 25. *Kinu* and *Uranami*, delayed by damage to the latter, departed at 1730hrs for Ormoc after the cruiser loaded 347 men and the destroyer 150. All the embarked troops were delivered to Ormoc early on October 26.

After unloading, *Kinu* and *Uranami* departed with three of the transports for Manila. Soon thereafter, at 1020hrs, *Kinu* and *Uranami* were attacked by aircraft from Escort Carrier Group Taffy 2. A total of 23 Avengers and 29 Wildcats from *Manila Bay* and *Natoma Bay* participated in the attack. A second wave from Taffy 1 added another 13 Avengers with torpedoes and 15 Wildcats. The American strikes caught up with the Japanese in the Visayan Sea only two hours out of Ormoc and launched repeated attacks. *Uranami* was heavily strafed again and was hit by a bomb in a boiler room, reducing her speed. A second bomb hit at 1110hrs, which caused flooding severe enough that the captain ordered the ship to be abandoned. *Uranami* sank just after noon; 103 of her crew were killed, and only 94 were rescued.

Destroyer *Uranami* under attack from escort carrier aircraft south of Masbate on October 26. The poor-quality gun camera image was taken by an aircraft from *Sangamon*. The destroyer sank after receiving bomb and rocket damage.

Kinu was hit by two bombs and later by a third that caused extensive hull damage aft and created fires. The cruiser was dead in the water at 1400hrs before sinking at 1745hrs southwest of Masbate Island. Another 83 men were killed and 51 wounded. For this minor victory, the Americans lost only an Avenger and a Wildcat. Over the course of the next three days, the two LSTs were also lost.

This little-known operation set a pattern for future Japanese reinforcement operations that extended into December. In spite of the fact that the Battle of Leyte Gulf resulted in a crippling defeat for the IJN, the Japanese decided to fight the decisive ground battle in the Philippines on Leyte, not Luzon. Another eight convoys were run to Leyte from Manila and other points to move four divisions to the island. In spite of heavy losses, the Japanese delivered an estimated 45,000 men and 10,000 tons of supplies and equipment to Leyte. This was a remarkable performance under the circumstances, but also ultimately futile and probably ill considered. It did though, as MacArthur feared, extend the ground campaign.

AFTERMATH

Both the battles of Surigao Strait and off Cape Engaño were resounding victories for the USN. Kinkaid and Oldendorf planned and fought a solid battle at Surigao Strait. The only imperfection on the American side was the lack of an aggressive follow-up that allowed most of Shima's force to escape.

The ledger for the Battle off Cape Engaño indicated another lopsided American victory. Ozawa's force had not been annihilated as Halsey had planned, but all four Japanese carriers were sunk. The sacrifice of the four carriers was a high price to pay, but it did open the door for Kurita to slip through San Bernardino Strait and eventually attack Kinkaid's escort carriers. This resulted in the heaviest USN losses of the battle—one escort carrier, two destroyers, one destroyer escort sunk, and some 1,900 casualties. In contrast, losses to TF 38 (one light carrier) and Oldendorf's forces at Surigao Strait (one destroyer damaged) were minor.

Halsey's chase to the north prevented him from achieving the decisive victory he had sought. Had he used more imagination, and embraced decentralized decision-making and execution, TF 38 could have engaged both Ozawa and Kurita and crushed both. Debating whether or not Halsey could have and should have engaged them both misses the point. The USN did gain a decisive victory at Leyte Gulf. Losses to the IJN forces covered in this book are detailed in Table 5.

Table 5: Losses suffered by the Second Diversion Attack Force, Nishimura Force, Main Body, and the Southwest Area Fleet Guard Force, October 22–27, 1944

Ship type	At start	Sunk	Severely damaged	Remaining
Carriers	4	4	N/A	0
Battleships	4	2	0	2
Heavy cruisers	4	1	1	2
Light cruisers	5	3	0	2
Destroyers	20	8	0	12
Total	**37**	**18**	**1**	**18**

Added to the losses suffered by the First Diversion Attack Force (one battleship, eight heavy cruisers sunk or heavily damaged, one light cruiser, and three destroyers), the total attrition to the IJN's remaining strength was calamitous. It rendered the IJN unable to conduct large-scale operations for the rest of the war.

In spite of heavy losses, Ozawa accomplished his mission. The IJN's other decoy force, Nishimura's, also performed to the best of its ability, but suffered near complete annihilation. Nishimura's force served its purpose by occupying the Seventh Fleet's surface force for the night of October 24/25 and making it expend much of its ordnance. Had the same forces been tasked to intercept the Kurita force as it entered the gulf, this would have been a significant factor. The Shima force contributed nothing to the mission, but at least survived largely intact.

Zuiho on fire and down by the stern after the third raid. Cruiser *Oyodo* is in the foreground.

Whatever losses the IJN suffered, it failed in its stated mission of stopping the invasion of Leyte. Even if Kurita had entered Leyte Gulf unmolested on the morning of October 25 and sunk every USN Liberty ship and LST present, his losses would have resulted in nothing more than a slight delay to American plans. Ironically, the IJN's greatest success around Leyte came after the battle when the USN failed to secure control of the seas around the island following its victory. As a result, the Japanese were able to reinforce their garrison on Leyte and managed to drag the battle into December.

This view of *Zuiho*, taken by an aircraft from *Franklin*, shows her condition after 1445hrs when she lost all power and came to a stop. The flight deck damage is visible, and the ship is heavily down by the stern. Within some 30 minutes of this photograph being taken, *Zuiho* sank with the loss of 215 men.

BIBLIOGRAPHY

Dull, Paul S., *A Battle History of the Imperial Japanese Navy (1941–1945)*, Naval Institute Press, Annapolis, MD (1978)

Falk, Stanley L., *Decision at Leyte*, W.W. Norton and Company, New York, NY (1966)

Field, James A., *The Japanese at Leyte Gulf: The Shō Operation*, Princeton University Press, Princeton, NJ (1947)

Friedman, Kenneth I., *Afternoon of the Rising Sun*, Presidio Press, Navato, CA (2001)

Halsey, William F. and Bryan, J., *Admiral Halsey's Story*, Zenger Publishing Co., Washington, DC (1947)

Hoyt, Edwin P., *The Battle of Leyte Gulf*, Weybright and Talley, New York, NY (1972)

Hughes, Thomas Alexander, *Admiral Bill Halsey*, Harvard University Press, Cambridge, MA (2016)

Ito, Masanori, *The End of the Imperial Japanese Navy*, W.W. Norton and Company, New York, NY (1962)

Japanese Monograph No. 82, *Philippines Area Naval Operations, Part I Jan.–Sep. 1944*, General Headquarters Supreme Commander for the Allied Powers (1947)

Japanese Monograph No. 84, *Philippines Area Naval Operations, Part II Oct.–Dec. 1944*, General Headquarters Supreme Commander for the Allied Powers (1947)

Lacroix, Eric and Wells, Linton, *Japanese Cruisers of the Pacific War*, Naval Institute Press, Annapolis, MD (1997)

Morison, Samuel Eliot, *History of United States Naval Operations in World War II, Volume XII, Leyte June 1944–January 1945*, Little, Brown and Company, Boston, MA (1974)

O'Hara, Vincent P., *The US Navy Against the Axis*, Naval Institute Press, Annapolis, MD (2007)

Potter, E.B., *Bull Halsey*, Naval Institute Press, Annapolis, MD (1985)

Prados, John, *Storm over Leyte*, NAL Caliber, New York, NY (2016)

Reynolds, Clark, *The Fast Carriers*, Naval Institute Press, Annapolis, MD (1992)

Sears, David, *The Last Epic Naval Battle*, Praeger, Westport, CT (2005)

Solberg, Carl, *Decision and Dissent*, Naval Institute Press, Annapolis, MD (1995)

Southwest Pacific Area Command, *Japanese Operations in the Southwest Pacific Area, Volume II, Part II*, Tokyo (1950)

Tully, Anthony P., *Battle of Surigao Strait*, Indiana University Press, Bloomington, IN (2009)

United States Strategic Bombing Survey (Pacific), *The Campaigns of the Pacific War*, United States Government Printing Office, Washington (1946)

United States Strategic Bombing Survey (Pacific), *Interrogations of Japanese Officials (Volume 1)*, United States Government Printing Office, Washington (n.d.)

Wheeler, Gerald R., *Kinkaid of the Seventh Fleet*, Naval Institute Press, Annapolis, MD (1996)

Willmott, H.P., *The Battle of Leyte Gulf*, Indiana University Press, Bloomington, IN (2005)

Woodward, C. Vann, *The Battle for Leyte Gulf*, W.W. Norton and Company, New York, NY (1947)

Websites:
www.combinedfleet.com

INDEX

Figures in **bold** refer to illustrations.